THE HOHOKAM

The School of American Research wishes to thank

the Inn at Loretto and Charlotte N. Gray

for their generous support of this book

The Authors

PATRICIA L. CROWN is an archaeologist and assistant professor of anthropology at Arizona State University.

DAVID E. DOYEL is an archaeologist who specializes in the American Southwest.

SUZANNE K. FISH is an ethnobotanist and research associate at the Arizona State Museum.

EMIL W. HAURY is an archaeologist and professor emeritus at the University of Arizona.

DOUGLAS W. SCHWARTZ is an archaeologist and president of the School of American Research.

HENRY D. WALLACE is a research archaeologist at Desert Archaeology, Inc., in Tucson.

DAVID R. WILCOX is curator of anthropology at the Museum of Northern Arizona in Flagstaff.

RICHARD B. WOODBURY is an archaeologist and professor emeritus at the University of Massachusetts at Amherst.

The HOHOKAM

Ancient People of the Desert

EDITED BY DAVID GRANT NOBLE

SCHOOL OF AMERICAN RESEARCH PRESS • SANTA FE • NEW MEXICO

SCHOOL OF AMERICAN RESEARCH PRESS
P.O. Box 2188, Santa Fe, New Mexico 87504-2188

Assistant Editor: Tom Ireland
Designer: Deborah Flynn Post
Cover Design: Pat Waganaar
Indexer: Douglas J. Easton
Printer: Southeastern Printing

Cover: Detail of the Sacaton Red-on-buff bowl shown on page 57. Colors have been added. *Frontispiece:* Ceramic figurines excavated from Snaketown. Courtesy Arizona State Museum, photograph by Helga Teiwes.

Library of Congress Cataloging-in-Publication Data:
The Hohokam : ancient people of the desert / edited by David Grant Noble. -- 1st ed.
       p. cm.
       Includes bibliographical references and index.
       ISBN 0-933452-29-2 (pbk.) : $10.95
       1. Hohokam culture. 2. Arizona--Antiquities. I. Noble, David Grant. II. School of American Research (Santa Fe, N.M.)
E99.H68H635 1991
979. 1'01--dc20
                                91-14113
                                CIP

Contents

Foreword

Traveling Through Time to the Desert Southwest

A TIME TRAVELER visiting the Sonoran desert region around Phoenix, Arizona, in the year A.D. 1100 would encounter a surprising and fascinating world. In this harsh, arid environment, dozens of small agricultural villages prospered in the major river valleys and along an intricate network of irrigation canals. The villagers, a people known to us as the Hohokam, labored in their fields of corn, beans, and squash, cultivated cotton and tobacco, and harvested the wild plants of the desert. They found time as well to create delicate shell carvings, turquoise mosaics, and beautifully painted red-on-buff pottery. Extensive trade relationships and elaborate ritual activities shaped their daily lives; in death, they were cremated or buried in pottery urns. Some of the villages were dominated by monumental earthworks—ceremonial ball courts and platform mounds that faced broad plazas and were surrounded by high palisades. The ball courts, along with vibrantly colored macaws and parrots and small copper bells, give clues to Hohokam's cultural links with the high civilizations of Mesoamerica to the south.

During this time period, the American Southwest was home to three other major prehistoric cultures. Best known are the Anasazi of the northern plateau country, creators of the magnificent architecture at Mesa Verde and Chaco Canyon. In

Pioneer-period figurines. Courtesy Arizona State Museum, photograph by Helga Teiwes.

the central mountains lived the Mogollon people, and to the west, along the Colorado River, the Hakataya. Of the four, the Hohokam are in many ways the most intriguing—in part because of the many questions that remain unanswered about the origins, rise to prominence, social complexity, extraordinary longevity, and ultimate demise of their society.

The Hohokam: Ancient People of the Desert delineates what is known about the Hohokam culture and examines some of these unsolved mysteries. David Doyel introduces the reader to Hohokam culture and its much-debated chronology, Suzanne Fish describes their mastery of the desert environment, and Richard Woodbury outlines the history of Hohokam archaeology. Hohokam craftsmen and their artistic legacy are appraised by Patricia Crown, and Henry Wallace looks at their rock art. David Wilcox uses evidence from public architecture and ritual artifacts to speculate on the nature of Hohokam religion. Finally, Emil Haury muses on the meaning of the Hohokam archaeological record in an epilogue to the volume.

Our knowledge of the prehistory of the Southwest is the result of only about a century of archaeological investigation, but an extraordinary amount of data has been collected in that time. I present this volume as a travel guide to another culture and another era—the Hohokam of prehistory—and leave you in the capable hands of those professional time travelers, the archaeologists of today.

Douglas Schwartz
President
School of American Research

THE HOHOKAM

The Hohokam

Ancient Dwellers of the Arizona Desert

David E. Doyel

T HE SONORAN DESERT of southern Arizona contains
a diverse community of native plants and animals, fertile soils, and major river systems. This environment, with its
long growing seasons, nourished Native Americans long before
Europeans stepped ashore in the New World. Recently, the
desert has experienced an influx of new residents and an accompanying economic boom. This phenomenon, however, is but the
most recent chapter in a millennia-old story.

Modern Americans generally know little about the Sonoran
Desert's first settlers. We were preceded in the area now called
Arizona by an aboriginal people known as the Hohokam. Archaeologists date the earliest sites of these pioneering desert dwellers
to around the time of Christ. By A.D. 700, the Hohokam were
thriving in numerous farming villages strung along the Salt, Gila,
and Santa Cruz rivers in the Phoenix Basin. Their culture
reached a climax between A.D. 1100 and 1400, after which, for
reasons still uncertain, it declined. By the time Europeans
explored southern Arizona in the late seventeenth century, the
Hohokam had gone, but not without writing an intriguing and
significant chapter in the prehistory of North America.

If the Anasazi Indians are most widely known for the magnificent masonry pueblos and cliff dwellings they built on the

Early photograph of Casa Grande Ruins. Courtesy Southwest Museum.

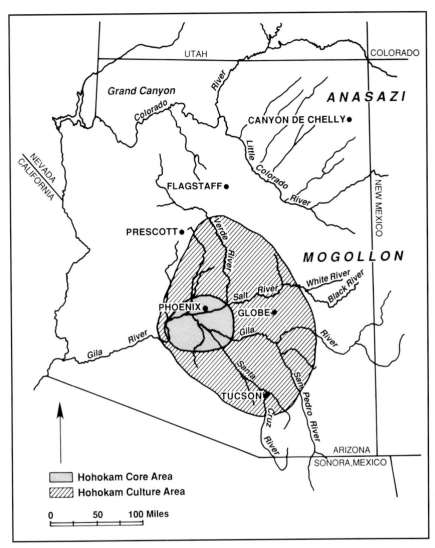

UTAH   COLORADO

Grand Canyon

A N A S A Z I

CANYON DE CHELLY•

NEVADA
CALIFORNIA

Colorado River

Little Colorado River

FLAGSTAFF•

NEW MEXICO

PRESCOTT•

M O G O L L O N

Verde River

White River
Black River

Salt River

PHOENIX•
GLOBE•

Gila

River

Gila River

Santa

San Pedro River

TUCSON•

Cruz

River

ARIZONA
SONORA,MEXICO

Hohokam Core Area
Hohokam Culture Area

0   50   100 Miles

Arizona, showing Hohokam culture area. Map by Katrina Lasko.

Colorado Plateau, the Hohokam should be equally noted for their sophisticated irrigation systems with which they grew cotton and tobacco along with the southwestern triad of corn, beans, and squash. They built large mounds in their villages and played ceremonial games in massive earthen "ball courts." The Hohokam were masters of desert survival, harvesting a variety of edible cactus and agave products. In the area of crafts, they made a distinctive red-on-buff pottery, wove colorful textiles, and created many wondrous items of stone, shell, and clay. Unlike their Anasazi neighbors to the north, they often cremated their dead.

The Hohokam lived near extensive trade routes ranging from the California coast to the Great Plains and from Mesoamerica to the Rocky Mountains. Buffalo and deer skins, sea shells, obsidian, rare minerals, textiles, salt, feathers, pottery, and other items were traded throughout this vast network. Some aspects of their culture connect the Hohokam with the high cultures of Mexico to the south, while other characteristics reflect a basic southwestern affinity. Thus, the Hohokam were positioned both geographically and culturally to play a unique role in the evolution of prehistoric southwestern societies.

But what do we really know about the Hohokam? Due primarily to a lack of wood in the Sonoran Desert that can be dated by tree-ring analysis, a firm chronology for the Hohokam civilization has proven to be a formidable challenge to archaeologists. Not only has it been hard to assign a starting date for Hohokam history, but considerable disagreement also exists in correlating the various Hohokam cultural periods to the Christian calendar. This author's chronology represents a compromise between extreme views.

The Phoenix Basin in south central Arizona, an area of roughly 4,000 square miles, was the Hohokam heartland. Its narrow valleys, sandwiched between rugged mountain ranges, were well watered by rivers and streams emanating from the high country to the north and east. Varying environmental conditions within their territory greatly affected Hohokam lifestyles. For example, in the San Pedro and Santa Cruz valleys, where rainfall was more abundant, they were able to dry-farm successfully. The aridity of the Phoenix Basin, on the other hand, necessitated construction of extensive canal systems. These canals, which led through the fertile flatlands and river terraces, comprised the most complex irrigation system ever constructed in aboriginal North America. The Hohokam also had an extensive trade network. They imported argillite, turquoise, and steatite from the northern districts through a network of satellite villages strung along the trade routes, which reached far beyond their own territory.

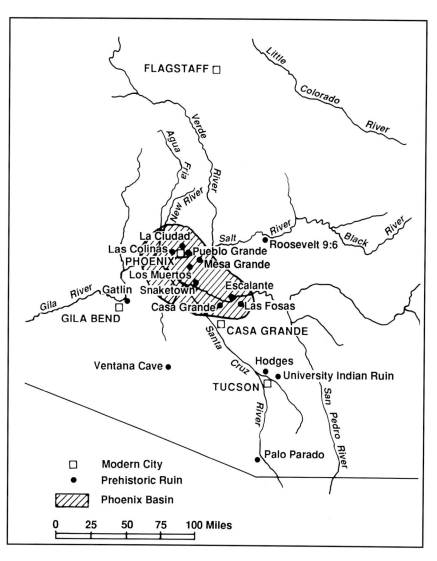

Major Hohokam sites. Map by Katrina Lasko.

HOHOKAM ORIGINS: 1000 B.C. TO A.D. 1

By 1,000 B.C., small bands of nomadic hunters and gatherers in Arizona—part of the continent-wide Archaic culture—began living in small hamlets in shallow pithouses built of wood, thatch, and mortar. Their possessions, as reflected in the archaeological record, were minimal: spears and knives for hunting, stone tools for grinding seeds, and "cloud-blower" pipes for use in rain and fertility ceremonies. They raised corn and squash by directing rainwater to their garden plots, and they buried their dead in the ground, curled up in the fetal position. Archaeologists, who have excavated in sites of these early southern-desert residents, call them the Cochise and view them as the probable ancestors of the Hohokam.

HOHOKAM CHRONOLOGY

YEAR	TRADITIONAL PERIODS	ALTERNATE PERIODS	PHASES	CHARACTERISTICS
1900 1850	Historic	Historic		American reservation system, cash economy, reduced agriculture.
1750			Blackwater	Spanish introduce livestock, wheat, metal tools. Warfare with Apaches.
1450		Protohistoric	Bachi	Development of historic Pimas and Tohono O'odham (Papagos). Father Kino gives mass at Casa Grande in 1694.
1350	Classic	Classic	Polvoron	Reduction of village size, ceremonial practices, and trade.
1250			Civano	Large irrigation-based communities. Big houses, compounds, polychrome pottery. Mounds include elite residences. Villages burned and some abandoned.
1150			Soho	Platform temple mounds and compounds dominant architectural style. Increasing social complexity.
1100			Santan	Many ancestral sites abandoned. Ball court system ends. New architectural styles developed. Polished Red Ware pottery popular. New ceremonies.
950	Sedentary	Late Formative	Sacaton	Expanded trade networks and irrigation. Increased village size.
850	Colonial		Santa Cruz	Artistic florescence. Cremation ritual elaborated.
800			Gila Butte	First ball courts built. Fewer figurines produced.
700			Snaketown	Canal irrigation. Increased village size. Red-on-buff pottery. First capped mounds.
600		Early Formative	Sweetwater	Expanding social interaction. Cotton production.
500			Estrella	Production of Red-on-gray decorated pottery and turquoise mosaic.
400 300	Pioneer		Vahki	Appearance of community lodges, village plazas, clay figurines, polished Red Ware pottery. Improved agriculture.
200 100 AD			Red Mountain	Appearance of small villages. Expansion into Phoenix Basin. First pottery made. Extended burials. Economy based on farming, hunting, and gathering.
BC 100 200 300		Western Archaic ↓		Agricultural beginnings. Houses, storage pits, baskets, and grinding tools present.

THE EARLY FORMATIVE PERIOD: A.D. 1 TO 700

Around A.D. 1, some Cochise groups began moving out of the mountains to settle in the lowlands along the rivers. Through the winters, they consumed and bartered agricultural produce grown over the summers. The culture of the lowland people continued to resemble that of the Cochise, except that they began living in villages more than double the size of the old Cochise mountain hamlets. They also began producing simple plain ware (Gila Plain) ceramic bowls and jars. These were the first Hohokam, a people who emphasized farming and agricultural production over foraging and probably experimented with such innovations as diversion dams, ditches, and levees. They also constructed large pit-houses at numerous sites, including Snaketown, where several of these structures encircled a large central plaza. Sometimes these large houses were more than five times the size of the average dwelling, which measured about 150 square feet. This development suggests the emergence of a new level of social organization among the Hohokam. We surmise that village chiefs lived in these big houses, which may also have been used as public meeting places to discuss important communal matters such as division of labor and resource sharing.

Gila Plain bowl. Courtesy Arizona State Museum, photograph by Helga Teiwes.

During this time, called the Early Formative or Pioneer period, the Hohokam also began producing a polished red ware pottery (Vahki Red). Later, they added a painted style combining red-on-gray color patterns with simple rectilinear designs (Estrella Red-on gray and Sweetwater Red-on-gray). Researchers believe they also may have traded shell, obsidian, and turquoise to such distant places as central Mexico, obtaining new crops such as cotton and beans in return.

New religious ideas and practices also may have traveled up the trade routes. We see evidence of this in the many ceremonial clay figurines archaeologists have found, including a collection of more than a thousand from the Snaketown site. These figurines (discussed later in this publication by both Patricia L. Crown and David R. Wilcox), may have been used in an agricultural fertility cult or in ancestor worship rituals. They also played a role in cremation burial rites.

Sweetwater Red-on-gray bowl. Courtesy Arizona State Museum, photograph by Helga Teiwes.

THE LATE FORMATIVE PERIOD: A.D. 700 TO 1100

Hohokam society continued to change. The first large earthen mounds that we associate with Hohokam culture appeared before A.D. 800. These slope-sided oval mounds, built of layers of accumulated trash and added soil, may have been used as dance platforms. Potters also developed a new style, a bright red-on-buff ware with diverse shapes and designs called Snaketown Red-on-buff. The Hohokam also began to cremate their dead, a practice that suggests religious change; ornate stone palettes, censors, and figurines often were placed in the graves. The archaeological record of this period shows other developments including canal irrigation, larger villages, population growth, more ceremonial activity, and increased trade. These innovations demonstrate a movement away from other southwestern cultural traditions and indicate a growing tribal identity.

Regionally, the practice of irrigation opened new agricultural lands on the terraces, removed from the river floodplains. Over 500 miles of main canals brought life-giving water to some 25,000 acres of fields in the Salt River Valley alone; hundreds of additional smaller ditches further expanded the potential to farm. Through time, Hohokam farmers consolidated the small local canals into much larger irrigation networks encompassing several villages and many square miles.

Some main canals were 50 feet wide at the bottom and 75 feet wide at the top. Archaeologists Paul and Suzanne Fish have estimated that it would have required one hundred men working one month a year for 420 years to construct the main canal systems of the Salt River Valley. Farmers probably needed to devote an equal amount of time to maintenance, construction of feeder ditches, and field preparation. In addition, it took many more hours of labor to build thousands of acres of agricultural terraces and dry-farming systems. The labor associated with canal construction and maintenance stimulated cooperation and economic ties among family groups and communities. The influx of additional people to supply growing labor demands may have further stimulated population growth.

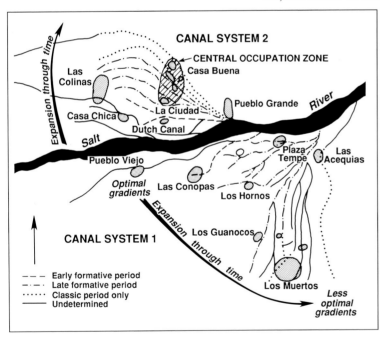

Hohokam irrigation system in the Salt River Valley through time. Courtesy Jerry Howard.

By around A.D. 800, the Hohokam had begun to build "ball courts," features that have greatly intrigued archaeologists and visitors to Hohokam ruins. The largest court ever built, at Snaketown, was over 16 feet high and nearly 200 feet long. Up to five hundred people could have stood on its massive adobe embankments. Scholars believe the Hohokam learned the ball game through their Mesoamerican contacts but developed their own version of the ritual, including an oval court.

Emil Haury standing in an excavated canal at Snaketown, 1964. Courtesy Arizona State Museum, photograph by Helga Teiwes.

Most major villages had ball courts, adjacent to plazas, where trade fairs and other activities such as socializing, gambling, and courtship could have taken place. The ball court network, which by A.D. 1050 included more than two hundred courts, was instrumental in regulating both local and long-distance trade. Archaeologists have found ball courts in non-Hohokam sites from Wupatki, north of Flagstaff, to Point of Pines, in east-central Arizona. Some of these sites also contain cremation burials. Were the Hohokam trying to introduce their religious concepts to their neighbors?

Hohokam traders developed extensive networks during this period. They even obtained goods from far to the south in Mesoamerica, including mosaic stone mirrors, marine shells, birds with ornate plumage, and copper bells. They also imported obsidian, chert, and quartz, from which artisans fashioned arrow and spear points and knife blades. Archaeologists have discovered a variety of Hohokam artifacts and trade goods in distant Anasazi and Mogollon sites, indicating a level of trade that probably brought wealth and power to sponsoring Hohokam village leaders. The Hohokam exported cotton, textiles, worked stone, salt, marine shell, pigments, agave, and other desert resources. In return, they received decorated pottery, turquoise, jet, and other materials.

The largest Hohokam villages of the Late Formative period had several hundred to a thousand people and exceeded 500 acres in area. Villages with ball courts were spaced evenly at about 3-mile intervals along irrigation canals, and some, such as

Snaketown, consisted of a ring of mounds and ball courts surrounding a great central plaza. Hohokam social organization also underwent significant changes during this period. Living areas consisted of groups of up to ten pithouses clustered around a small courtyard. Clusters of such house groups shared outside facilities, including cemeteries, large cooking ovens, and trash mounds. From excavations at Hohokam sites, we can also deduce that their society had developed a privileged class of families, from the presence of large houses containing items of wealth and rich cremation burials located nearby.

THE CLASSIC PERIOD: A.D. 1100 TO 1450

Sometime between A.D. 1050 and 1100, the abandonment of Snaketown and other ancestral towns marked the beginning of a new era in Hohokam history. Some craft arts declined, such as stone palettes and clay figurines, and traditional ceremonial practices began to disappear. Some communities stopped cremating their dead and began burying them with a new polished red ware pottery (Gila Red). The rejection of the old ways and the appearance of new social customs are further underscored by a shift from ball courts to large earthen platform mounds as the dominant theme in monumental architecture. After A.D. 1100 or so, few ball courts were built, and mounds became larger and more common than in earlier periods.

By A.D. 1200, a traveler entering a Hohokam village would have been likely to see residential areas consisting of numerous clusters of houses, each enclosed by a rectangular compound wall made of adobe. These compounds were clustered around one or more centrally located platforms, also enclosed by a wall. A small temple stood on top of the platform. Platform mounds are known to exist at fifty sites in the region. Some of

Top: Plan of the large Classic-period town of Los Muertos and the associated irrigation system. Redrawn from maps by Emil Haury and David Gregory.

Bottom: Artist's reconstruction of a Classic-period residential compound, after a drawing by Ben Mixon.

LOS MUERTOS

Ditch

Ditch

Ditch

Main Canal

Meters

0   200

■ Platform mound and compound
□ Other compound
◎ Trash/burial mound
⬭ Reservoir

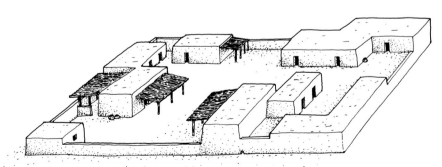

them, such as at Mesa Grande and Pueblo Grande, contain up to 32,000 cubic yards of fill. The mounds were probably built in phases, perhaps following a calendrical cycle, with construction costs spread over a number of generations. The Pueblo Grande mound in Phoenix, could have taken one hundred men working one month a year for twenty-four years to build.

While some older villages continued into the new era, many new villages also appeared. Some, such as Pueblo Grande and Los Muertos, were inhabited by as many as two thousand people, but most villages were probably smaller. By A.D. 1300, some elite families in Hohokam towns seem to have expressed their new-found power by building their homes on top of the large platform mounds. The final evolution of the plat-

Artist's conception of big houses built on earthen mounds after A.D. 1300 and lived in by members of elite lineages. The mounds were sometimes the scene of ceremonies. Drawing by John Joha in collaboration with David Doyel.

form mound architectural tradition can be seen at Casa Grande Ruins National Monument, near Coolidge. The bottom floor of this four-story house was a 6-foot-high earthen platform. Its occupants probably used it as a warehouse and astronomical observatory as well as their residence. Most Hohokam villagers did not live in such high style, but built small adobe dwellings or pithouses.

By A.D. 1300, the Hohokam were making much less of their distinctive red-on-buff pottery in favor of a highly polished red ware with a glossy black interior, known as Salt Red. Potters also began producing a new style of painted red, black, and white ware we have named Salado Polychrome. This pottery became popular throughout much of the Southwest, including Casas Grandes, a large town and trading center in northern Chihuahua, Mexico.

Ceremonies conducted during the Classic period seem to have been less public than during earlier times. The compounds, mounds, and walled plazas all suggest an emphasis on privacy and social status. At the same time, village leaders signaled their rank by adorning themselves with exotic items such as turquoise mosaic, worked marine shells, and bright feathers. Their houses, built on the high mounds, were brightly painted with icons and symbols to display their power and validate the social order.

THE TRANSITION TO HISTORIC TIMES

By A.D. 1400, calamity seems to have struck the Hohokam world. Many of the once-thriving towns were stripped of their material goods and put to the torch; other villages appear to have been abandoned more gradually. Numerous explanations have been proposed for this abandonment. Environmental causes (flood, soil salinization, and deteriorating climate) lead the list. Cultural

Pima man standing in front of a Pima round house built around 1915 and adjoining Snaketown. Courtesy Arizona State Museum, photograph by Emil Haury.

factors also may have played a part, including internal warfare, cessation of trade, shifting centers of power, and domination by Casas Grandes located several hundred miles to the southeast. Some scholars hold that the Classic Hohokam culture extended beyond 1600, only to meet its demise through introduced European diseases. As yet, however, no reliable archaeological evidence has been uncovered to support this claim. We do know that when Father Eusebio Francisco Kino first said mass at Casa

Grande in 1694, this great village already lay in ruins.

Archaeologists have traditionally maintained that the Hohokam were the ancestors of the Pima Indians, who were living in the Sonoran Desert at the time of the Spanish *entrada*. Indeed, recent excavations in the Phoenix Basin have revealed simple brush and adobe-covered structures dating from about 1375 to 1450 that resemble those of the historic Pimas. Many other similarities link the Hohokam and the Pimas, including council houses, public plazas, ball games, ceramic types, and numerous subsistence practices. Striking parallels in burial practices also exist.

One key to understanding the history of the Phoenix Basin lies in population reconstruction. The seventeenth-century Pima population in this region was about 5,000 people, a drop from an estimated 40,000 to 80,000 two centuries earlier. Population loss of this magnitude certainly would have drastically altered Hohokam society and culture, possibly resulting in the much less complex lifestyle that characterized the Pima Indians.

Interestingly, Pima Indian legends and oral history provide a somewhat different story of the disappearance of the Hohokam, which questions the Hohokam-Pima cultural continuum. Legend holds that the mound sites were occupied by wicked or powerful men called *civanos* (chiefs). Late in prehistory, ancestral Pima people from the east entered the Phoenix Basin and destroyed the *civanos* or drove them toward the Colorado River to the west. Warfare and migration would certainly help to explain the dramatic drop in population between 1400 and 1700. These legends challenge modern anthropologists to better familiarize themselves with the oral traditions of the desert dwellers and find ways to evaluate them using archaeological methods.

Between 1750 and 1870, the Gila Pimas acquired horses and began growing irrigated wheat. This introduced Old World crop provided them with a new and prolific winter food source. At the same time, the horse helped promote a highly integrated militaristic society to combat invading Apaches. After 1870, Apache depredations were quelled. However, new problems for the Pimas arose when Mexican and Anglo-American immigrants cut off the life-giving flow of the Gila River. Pima fields to the west of Florence dried up, agriculture declined, and the Pimas began to feel the strong acculturative pressures of the reservation system.

THE HOHOKAM IN SOUTHWESTERN CONTEXT

The great increase in archaeological research in the Arizona desert in recent years has provided critical evidence for evaluating Hohokam history. Scholars generally agree today that the Hohokam evolved from an earlier local hunting and gathering culture, a view that questions the once popular theory that the Hohokam immigrated into the area from some unknown location in Mexico.

A modern canal known as the Santan Ditch. Scientists hypothesize that this canal is flowing on the course of a prehistoric Hohokam canal. Courtesy Arizona State Museum, photograph by Helga Teiwes, 1965.

There is still much to be learned about the cultural relationships of the Hohokam to other southwestern traditions. Although their earliest beginnings suggest cultural patterns similar to those of the Anasazi and Mogollon, they soon acquired many attributes linking them to cultures far to the south. One must wonder whether or not the rise and fall of powerful Mesoamerican states such as Teotihuacán, Tula, and those along the northwest coast of Mexico sent ripples throughout the northern territories. What new ideas and customs did Mesoamerican traders and emissaries introduce to the Hohokam world? More research may help clarify these points and throw light on the relationships between the Hohokam of the Phoenix Basin and the people of Casas Grandes, some 350 miles to the southeast.

In his recent book, *Cadillac Desert*, Marc Reisner concludes that the mysterious disappearance of the remarkable Hohokam culture was ultimately linked to water: "They either had too little or used too much." Such speculation is intuitively satisfying. The average summer temperature in the Phoenix Basin is 94 degrees, and annual rainfall is only 7 inches, much of it coming in the form of violent storms. Desert soils also became salt laden and waterlogged from prolonged irrigation, a problem familiar to modern-day farmers in the region. Ultimately, the Hohokam may have become victims of their own limited technology, which, despite its successes, could not control the rivers during periods of extreme fluctuation.

Further explorations of these interpretations currently drive a new generation of archaeologists, bolstered by a tremendous surge in development funding brought on by the recent immigration of new people into the Sonoran Desert. Whether or not the Hohokam ever really mastered their desert environment, their long survival was an amazing achievement—one to be envied by modern residents of the region. Like the mythical phoenix reborn from its own ashes, new life surges in the modern cities and canals built upon the abandoned ruins of the ancient Hohokam civilization.

The Desert World
of the **Hohokam**

Suzanne K. Fish

OHOKAM COUNTRY in southern Arizona is marked
by low rainfall, high temperatures, and few sources of
permanent water. Although hot and dry conditions prevail
throughout, hardy Hohokam farmers settled even the areas of
more extreme climate. The prehistorically populous Phoenix
Basin, for example, receives only about 7.5 inches of rain per
year and experiences an average of 90 days at or above 100
degrees. In spite of this harsh environment, the Hohokam

A view of the Sonoran Desert. Photograph by Matts Myhrman, 1990.

Tohono O'odham woman harvesting saguaro fruit. Photograph by Suzanne Fish.

prospered for more than 1,500 years. How they achieved this long-term success by gathering the natural bounty of the desert and farming in the valleys is one of the most intriguing chapters in the story of these Indians.

Rather than a flat desert expanse, Hohokam territory consists of generally linear and parallel basins bordered by low, discontinuous mountain chains, which only occasionally include higher peaks with winter snowfall and conifer forests. Gentle slopes rise from the valley floors and become steeper near the bordering mountains. The elevations of most valleys range between 700 and 2,500 feet above sea level.

THE SONORAN DESERT

To describe the environment of the Hohokam is to describe the Sonoran Desert. Biologists divide arid portions of the southwestern United States and adjacent northwestern Mexico into several distinct deserts on the basis of characteristic plant species. A limited number of shrubs predominate in the Chihuahuan Desert to the east, the Great Basin Desert to the north, and the Mohave Desert to the west, but the Sonoran Desert is noted for the greater variety and larger size of its vegetation. Tall columnar cacti and desert trees of moderate size are common. Because both summer and winter have rainy seasons, plants do not have to endure dry spells lasting most of the year. Consequently, a greater diversity and abundance of plant resources was available to the Hohokam than to prehistoric peoples of adjacent desert areas.

The northeastern portion of the Sonoran Desert, which was inhabited by the Hohokam, has two major categories of vegetation. Lower Colorado River vegetation, with a high proportion of shrubs, is found in the relatively hotter and drier valleys as well as in the arid western sector of the state. Creosote bush and bursage are widespread, but saltbush is also common in portions of the Gila Valley subject to occasional flooding. Arizona Upland vegetation typifies upper basin slopes, low mountains, and the somewhat cooler and moister reaches of Hohokam occupation to the north, east, and south. Leguminous trees such as palo verde, ironwood, mesquite, and acacia combine with shrubs, ocotillo, saguaro cactus, cholla, prickly pear, and other succulents to create diversified and luxuriant desert landscapes.

Smaller desert animals live on the low, hot basin floors. Cottontail rabbits and jackrabbits, ground squirrels, pocket gophers, pack rats and other native rats, mice, lizards, and snakes are common. Pronghorn antelope occur widely in areas with good grass cover. Mule deer, white-tailed deer, and bighorn sheep are most numerous on upper basin slopes and in mountain borders, although their current elevational ranges are more restricted than they were in the past. The javelina, or collared peccary, which was not present prehistorically, spread northward into southern Arizona after the Hohokam era. Predators include coyotes, bobcats, and mountain lions. Dove and quail are typical desert game birds. Before the twentieth century, muskrat and beaver lived along segments of larger streams with permanent water and in the vicinity of *ciénagas* or marshes. These habitats, sharply reduced in modern times, also supported a variety of fish and waterfowl.

Plants and animals thrive along desert watercourses, but rivers with year-round flow afford the richest and most extensive floodplains. Cottonwood, willow, reed, and cattail mark the dampest locations. Groves of towering mesquite trees grow where deep roots can reach the water table. Shrubs such as saltbush and annual plants such as grasses and amaranths are concentrated in dense stands. Rivers support unique species and increase the density and productivity of plants and animals that are also found in other parts of the desert. When the Salt and Gila rivers flowed perennially through drier desert sectors, lush bands of growth along the floodplains helped to compensate for sparser human resources elsewhere.

WATER SOURCES OF THE DESERT

Life-giving rains come to the Sonoran Desert from separate weather systems over the Pacific Ocean and the Gulf of Mexico. In the winter, frontal systems from the west and north deliver gentle, long-lasting rainfall over broad regions. Summer rains from the southeast tend to fall as short, intense thunderstorms affecting areas no more than several miles in diameter. These storms cause rapid surface runoff, in contrast to winter rains, which are better able to infiltrate and moisten the soil. Winter precipitation plays a greater role in maintaining flow in the Salt and Gila rivers and in springs and streams of desert mountains. Other rivers in this region flow most strongly after summer rains.

Salt River in flood in 1888. Today, dams block its flow. Courtesy Arizona Historical Society Library.

High temperatures and low rainfall limit the natural availability of water for drinking in southern Arizona. In the past, human settlements had to be established within reasonable walking distance of a stream or spring. The need for domestic water clustered settlements along the floodplain of the major river in a basin and the flanks of mountain ranges. However, from the accounts of early Spaniards in Arizona, it is clear that all villages of that time were not located immediately adjacent to a permanently flowing watercourse or year-round spring. Particularly during the dry, hot period preceding midsummer rains, when seasonal sources failed, water might be obtained by walking several miles from dwellings. The Hohokam also devised means for prolonging the availability of seasonal water and supplying locations at some distance from natural sources. Canals transported water to villages and fields as far as ten miles inland from the channels of major rivers. In addition, the Indians dug wells where the water table was high and built earthen-banked reservoirs of various sizes filled by canal or diverted surface runoff.

HUNTING AND GATHERING IN THE DESERT

Archaeologists frequently recover charred plant parts, pollen, and animal bones in excavations of archaeological sites and are thus able to identify the foods, raw materials for crafts and building, and fuel used by the Hohokam. However, the manner in which the Hohokam procured and prepared these resources is only occasionally suggested in the archaeological record. Archaeologists are sometimes able to reconstruct prehistoric subsistence practices by observing the ways in which later Indian groups used similar resources and environments. The Pimas and the Tohono O'odham (Papagos) of southern Arizona, speakers of related Piman languages, are generally regarded as the groups most directly descended from the Hohokam. Historic documents of the Spanish, Mexican, and Anglo periods are sources of comparative information, as are more recent accounts of Piman lifeways and those of other Native Americans. Knowledge of historic agriculture among Indian groups of the Southwest further aids in understanding the prehistoric crop varieties and agricultural technology that allowed the Hohokam to farm in the desert.

The Sonoran Desert offers a generous bounty to hunters and gatherers. Although few useful plants have been directly identified from remains in Hohokam sites, more than 250 species are known to have been used as foods by Indians of southern Arizona during historic times. The mesquite and several other trees of the legume family produce edible seed pods. Cacti and other succulents, including yucca and agave, or century plant, provide foods and fibers. Nutritious seeds and small, fleshy fruits can be harvested from a variety of shrubs. Even the ephemeral plants that live for short periods during rainy seasons furnish plentiful seeds and leafy parts that can be eaten as greens. Important plant resources do not all grow or ripen simultaneously. Different species become available from early spring through the fall, and the same species may mature somewhat later at higher elevations. Many resources can be processed and stored for a year or more.

Most Hohokam had ready access to the tall saguaro cactus, which grows most densely on upper valley slopes and mountain edges. Plentiful fruits, ripening at the tops of the cacti in June and early July, were a particularly favored food. For the Pimans, the new year begins with the saguaro harvest, a festive occasion marked by much eating and drying of fresh fruits, and the making of saguaro wine. Fruits contain a sugary pulp, and syrup made from boiling either fresh or dried pulp was a common article of historic trade. When separated, saguaro seeds can be eaten raw or ground into meal.

Baked agave hearts are still prized as a food in Sonora, Mexico, today. Photograph by Suzanne Fish.

Above: Prickly pear cactus in fruit. Photograph by Matts Myhrman. Below: Mesquite beans. Photograph by David Noble.

The slopes of Sonoran Desert basins contain two other cacti important to the Hohokam: the closely related cholla, with its cylindrical leaves and joints; and the prickly pear, with its flattened pads. The Indians could collect large quantities of unopened cholla buds in the late spring to bake in preheated pit ovens. In this way, they obtained a vegetable furnishing calcium to a diet otherwise low in that nutrient. They also dried cholla buds for storage and later preparation, first soaking or boiling them. The Pimans consider the fruits and young joints of most cholla species less appetizing than the buds, but these are the most desirable parts of prickly pear. Prickly pear fruits are eaten fresh or dried. Cooked strips of young pads are eaten as a green vegetable after careful removal of spines.

Both the Hohokam and later Pimans commonly ate mesquite beans, gathered along drainages and on slopes. Individual trees do not bear at the same rate every year, but stands of larger trees along watercourses produce abundant and predictable mid- to late-summer harvests. Beans can be pounded into a meal and stored up to two years. Studies have shown that among the Seri Indians, who live to the south and west of Hohokam territory, one man collecting and two women pounding and winnowing might average 90 pounds of processed meal per day. Raw or parched whole beans were often stored in special granaries made of rough basketry.

The Hohokam also consumed small, energy-rich seeds from a wide range of desert annuals such as grasses, amaranths, and tansy mustard. Most annual plants in the Sonoran Desert begin growing in response to winter or summer rains. Tansy mustard and wild barley grass are winter annuals, whereas most amaranth species appear in summer. The young leaves and stems of annuals, often the same species providing seeds, were eaten seasonally and sometimes dried. Areas around Hohokam villages and fields may have been among the most productive for gathering many annual species, which tend to sprout densely in open patches of disturbed ground. Various historic Indian groups permitted or even encouraged desirable annuals to grow in fields, where supplemental water for crops also assured their supply.

The Hohokam consumed less meat than plant foods. Nevertheless, large quantities of jackrabbit and cottontail bone are present in most archaeological sites, as are bones of various rodents and birds. Pimans have eaten pack rats, gophers, ground squirrels, and other rodents. Although these smaller species could be hunted and trapped at a distance from settlements, animals attracted to agricultural fields for food and water were particularly convenient prey. Deer remains are less common in Hohokam sites, but a single deer would have provided a significant amount of meat. Bighorn sheep and other large animals were an even rarer prey. Delicate fish bones and scales, found occasionally with the most painstaking archaeological recovery methods, confirm early Spanish accounts, which indicate that the Pimans fished in major rivers.

HOHOKAM AGRICULTURE

Like other aboriginal farming groups of North America, the Hohokam relied heavily on corn, beans, and squash. Most of these kinds of crops originated to the south, in Mexico, before being acquired by the Hohokam, although tepary beans may have been brought under cultivation in the Sonoran Desert. These prehistoric farmers developed strains of beans that were heat, drought, and insect resistant, and quickly maturing corn varieties that avoided the risks of an extended growing period in the desert. Their beans included tepary beans, common beans, lima beans, and jack beans. They also raised squash and pumpkin, from which the flesh and seeds were eaten, and bottle gourds, which were used as containers. In addition, cotton was grown as a source of textile fiber and for the oily cotton seeds, which were toasted and eaten.

The Hohokam added to the productivity of their agriculture by transplanting selected desert perennials such as agave or century plant and possibly cholla. A succulent with stiff, pointed leaves growing in a rosette, the agave stores carbohydrates over its lifetime of approximately ten years for a single and final flowering event. When baked in a pit, stored nutrients in the plant base are converted to a sweet, pithy food. Fibers in the leaves can be extracted to make string, rope, nets, and coarse cloth. Fermented agave is the base for tequila, mescal, and other Mexican alcoholic beverages, but there is no evidence that the Hohokam used agave this way. These drought-adapted plants were grown in mulches of piled rock and on low terraces lacking sufficient water for crops such as corn. Agaves were

Drought-resistant, fast-maturing corn adapted for desert farming. Photograph by Suzanne Fish.

probably also planted in borders along the edges of better, watered fields.

Versatile Hohokam farming practices permitted widespread reliance on agricultural products, but water to supplement rainfall was necessary everywhere for successful crops of corn, beans, and squash. The Hohokam maintained impressive canal systems for this purpose on the Salt and Gila rivers. They also practiced floodwater farming, making use of water generated by storms. When larger drainages from mountains or upper basins reach flatter slopes near the valley floor, their rate of flow becomes slower, and suspended particles of soil are deposited in stream beds. This process builds accumulations of fine soils called alluvial fans. Water in broad, shallow channels on alluvial fans could be easily deflected onto fields at the sides. The Hohokam cultivated many floodwater fields outside the Phoenix Basin. On middle to upper basin slopes, they also built brush and stone walls to direct surface runoff onto terraces, grids, and piles of stone that promoted water infiltration and conservation. An added benefit of water delivered to fields by floodwater and runoff techniques was a natural fertilizer of suspended topsoil and organic debris.

OTHER DESERT RESOURCES
The Hohokam were faced with a continuing need for fuel and construction materials in a desert environment where wood could be quickly exhausted near villages. Supply problems must have been especially pronounced for large, long-term sites such as Snaketown and Pueblo Grande, in the densely occupied Phoenix Basin, where trees are naturally sparse. Archaeologists find remains of mesquite, palo verde, ironwood, and woody shrubs in fuel charcoal. Riparian trees and driftwood from floods on large drainages were also burned. Hornos or pit ovens, often shared by several households, were dug into the earth—a cooking method that conserved heat. Foods placed in these pits with hot rocks or coals were covered and left to bake slowly for many hours. Other efficient uses of fuel included parching of seeds and grains by shaking them with hot coals in baskets or ceramic containers.

The Hohokam used desert trees of basin slopes and drainages for roof beams but had difficulty finding long, straight

trunks. Alternative materials such as saguaro ribs and ocotillo branches served as lesser supports. Reed, cattail, grasses, and brush covered walls and roofs. For the largest adobe structures, particularly those within the special precincts of platform mounds at important sites, the Hohokam carried juniper, pine, and other conifer beams down from the mountains.

Pima dwelling, ca. 1938, demonstrating use of saguaro ribs as a building material. Courtesy Arizona Historical Society Library.

CONCLUSIONS

Plants and animals of the desert made up an important part of the Hohokam economy, even in the largest sites with the longest settlement histories. Wise use must have been necessary to ensure continued supplies of these resources. However, growing populations in later Hohokam times must have become increasingly dependent on harvests of irrigated, floodwater, and runoff fields. Archaeologists do not yet know all the details of how the Hohokam made their living from this arid country. To better answer this question, study in recent years has turned to remains of plants and animals used for food, evidence of farming techniques in ancient fields, and the small scatters of artifacts left behind by hunting and gathering expeditions.

Skills for desert dwelling enabled the Hohokam to support larger populations and to occupy a broader range of environments than the Indians of southern Arizona during the later historic era. They persisted in the face of a harsh and unpredictable climate and its fluctuations over time. Perhaps the best tribute to their unique accomplishments lies in the remains of once-thriving villages on dry basin slopes, where only a handful of cattle graze today.

A Brief History of Hohokam Archaeology

Richard B. Woodbury

*T*HE ARCHAEOLOGICAL study of the Hohokam Indians began in the 1880s, long before the term Hohokam was known by European-Americans, when southern Arizona was still a frontier, and the science of archaeology in North America was in its infancy. Frank Hamilton Cushing, who first systematically investigated the archaeology of the Arizona desert, had been interested in the Indian past ever since he was a boy, collecting arrowheads in the woods near his home in upstate New York. Soon he was experimenting with flaking his own arrowheads; he also made himself an Indian costume and a wigwam for his private retreat. In his adult career he became a brilliant and eccentric scholar and a skilled scientific entrepreneur. By the 1880s, he already was famous for his four years' residence at the pueblo of Zuni in the dual roles of adopted Zuni Indian and Smithsonian Institution ethnologist, and in 1886 he brought a group of Zuni friends to the eastern United States. Their tour included a stay at the summer home of the wealthy Boston philanthropist Mary Hemenway, where Cushing interested her in supporting archaeological research, beginning with the antecedents of the Zunis. This collaboration quickly led to the Mary Hemenway Southwestern Archaeological Expedition, a multiyear, well-organized, interdisciplinary effort and the best funded and best staffed archaeological investigation of the southwestern United States up to that time. Arriving at Zuni Pueblo in January 1887, Cushing realized that

Frank Hamilton Cushing, ca. 1882. Courtesy Museum of New Mexico, neg. no. 59625. Photograph by D. F. Mitchell.

Snaketown excavations in 1935. Courtesy Arizona State Museum.

it was far too wintry for digging there and immediately led his expedition south to the Salt River Valley, where he chose for excavation a large group of mounds, which he named El Pueblo de los Muertos.

Unfortunately, the results of Cushing's fifteen months of excavation were not reported in print until more than fifty years later. Many of the field records were missing, although some have since been found. The specimens had ended up in the Peabody Museum at Harvard, and their description and analysis provided the basis for a 1934 doctoral dissertation by Emil W. Haury, the first of his major contributions to Hohokam archaeology. Haury did his first archaeological work in 1925 with Byron Cummings of the University of Arizona ("the Dean"), excavating at Cuicuilco in Mexico. Five years later, he began a lifetime career in southwestern archaeology, first as assistant director of Gila Pueblo, a research center in Globe, Arizona, and then as director of the Arizona State Museum and head of the anthropology department at the University of Arizona. During the next half century he became the Southwest's leading archaeologist, and in retirement he is still continuing his research and writing.

Alfred Vincent Kidder and Emil W. Haury at the University of Arizona archaeological field school, Point of Pines. Courtesy Arizona State Museum, photograph by E. B.Sayles.

After Cushing's pioneering work, interest in the archaeology of the Arizona desert lapsed for several decades. Its relatively unknown ruins were far less impressive at first sight than the masonry pueblos and cliff dwellings of the Colorado Plateau. Also, most archaeologists conducted field work in the summer, and the mesa country was far more appealing than the blistering desert. Thus, Hohokam archaeology lagged far behind that of the northern Southwest.

The term *Hohokam* for the ancient people of the Arizona desert was suggested in 1908 by Frank Russell, who learned the word from the Pima Indians whom he was studying. He wrote that they told him it meant "those who have gone," but "all used up" is a more literal translation. The term only came into use archaeologically in the 1930s.

EARLY TWENTIETH-CENTURY INVESTIGATIONS

Meanwhile, archaeologists gradually began to realize that the past culture of the Arizona desert was distinctly different from the long-familiar Pueblo culture of the north and not merely a variant of it. In 1906–1908, Jesse Walter Fewkes, better known for his digging in the Hopi country and Mesa Verde, excavated in the vast ruins of Casa Grande, near present-day Coolidge, where the only multistory adobe "great house" survived. He not only endeavored to have it protected as a national monument but also observed in his 1912 report that the "Gila Valley culture" was quite different from the northern or Pueblo culture. In 1924, A. V. Kidder published his masterful *An Introduction to the Study of Southwestern Archaeology*, the first archaeological synthesis of any New World area. In this work he, too, recognized the distinctiveness of what he called the Lower Gila area, with its "aberrant" Red-on-buff pottery, unlike anything else in the Southwest. A. L. Kroeber went a step further in 1928, proposing the name "Gila-Sonoran" as a major prehistoric cultural unit, distinct from the Pueblo culture of the Colorado Plateau.

Odd Halseth (left), Neil Judd, and two aviators of the U. S. Army Air Corps. Courtesy San Diego Museum of Man.

In the late 1920s, when very little archaeological information had yet been gathered from the desert area, a few significant investigations were made. In 1925, Erich Schmidt of the American Museum of Natural History made the first stratigraphic excavations in the Hohokam area at Pueblo Grande and La Ciudad, in the Salt River Valley, thus laying the foundation for a chronology of Hohokam development. Equally important was the 1929 aerial photographic survey of still-visible ancient canals made by Neil

M. Judd of the Smithsonian Institution and Odd S. Halseth, city of Phoenix archaeologist. The resulting photographs by the U.S. Army Air Corps preserve for us today a wealth of information that would otherwise have been lost as urban growth and agriculture obliterated the evidence of prehistoric irrigation. Also in the 1920s, Omar A. Turney of Phoenix compiled his own maps of Hohokam irrigation along the Salt River, work that was carried further in the next few decades by Frank Midvale. Yet, nobody had undertaken a broad reconstruction of southern Arizona prehistory comparable to what had been achieved for the Colorado Plateau area.

GLADWIN, GILA PUEBLO, AND SNAKETOWN

In 1927, a new actor appeared on the archaeological stage— Harold S. Gladwin, who had sold his seat on the New York Stock Exchange, moved to California, and converted by Kidder, become an enthusiastic avocational archaeologist: "My archaeological career began at 10:30 a.m., August 24th [1924], on the road from Cameron to Oraibi, when Dr. Kidder pointed to a low mound and said, 'There's a ruin.' It looked like a prairie dog's burrow to me, and I demanded to be shown. Sure enough, the mound was covered with sherds, and by the time we had made a collection my future course was set." This was a time when professional training in archaeology was available in only a few universities, so learning by doing and taking part in the excavations of others was often the only training a beginner could find. Gladwin, Cushing, Fewkes, Judd, F. W. Hodge, and many others advanced in this way to a status equaling that of the newly emerging professionally trained group.

After a short apprenticeship with the Southwest Museum in Los Angeles, Gladwin established his own research center, Gila Pueblo, in Globe, Arizona. Kidder advised him that the Lower Gila "held greater possibilities [for research] than any other area," and Gladwin focused his attention on it for the next three decades. After extensive and careful surveys, he and his archaeological staff, beginning with Haury, E. B. Sayles, Monroe Amsden, and Frank Midvale, failed to find an origin outside southern Arizona for the Red-on-buff Culture, as he then called it. In 1934 they therefore turned their attention to one of the largest sites in the Gila-Salt Basin—Snaketown. Gladwin personally financed and organized its excavation, and Haury directed

Harold S. Gladwin, age ninety-five. Courtesy Arizona State Museum.

the field work. Gladwin delighted in challenging accepted ideas with brilliant, sometimes eccentric alternatives, but he insisted on thorough, high-quality excavation. This, Haury and his staff accomplished excellently.

The resulting report *Excavations at Snaketown: Material Culture,* a masterpiece of detailed recording and analysis, established for the first time a comprehensive chronology of Hohokam culture. This sequence, which would be argued about for the next half century, was firmly based on stratigraphy, but the report's findings on the age of the Snaketown settlement depended on Colorado Plateau sherds found there. Because these sherds, probably evidence of trade, could be dated only approximately and had to be correlated with deposits of the various phases of Hohokam occupation, there was plenty of room for differing interpretations. Although tree-ring dating for pueblo ruins was a well-established practice, the burned wood at Snaketown was not suitable for dating, and the estimated dates could not be confirmed by this method. After only a few years, Gladwin changed his interpretation drastically, deciding that the Hohokam sequence began in A.D. 600 instead of 300 B.C. and each phase lasted fifty years instead of two hundred. Haury still argued for long phases, but in the years ahead, several other archaeologists also proposed new chronologies, usually starting the first period of the Hohokam culture, known as the Pioneer period, much later than 300 B.C.

Fortunately, the content of the Hohokam culture at Snaketown was far more firmly defined than its chronology. The excavations turned up evidence of a long occupation of the site; distinctive house types; irrigation canals; and many kinds of utilitarian and other artifacts, including shell jewelry, beautifully carved paint palettes, simple but attractive clay figurines, and the long sequence of distinctive pottery styles that had been the first clue to Hohokam uniqueness.

Meanwhile, Gladwin and Haury successfully persuaded other archaeologists that the innovative and useful scheme of southwestern cultural chronology proposed and agreed on in 1927 at the first Pecos Conference needed drastic modification, especially the addition of the Hohokam. Gladwin invited some twenty leading southwestern archaeologists to Gila Pueblo in April 1931 and presented them with a set of recommendations for changes in the nomenclature and relationships of prehistoric southwestern cultural units. Emil Haury conveyed these new ideas, including the name Hohokam for the prehistoric desert culture, to the Pecos Conference that summer and was able to have them accepted, though not without some initial skepticism. Haury recalls that Frank H. H. Roberts, then one of the Southwest's most respected younger archaeologists, turned to him after Haury had used the new term in reporting on recent excavations and said quietly, "That's a lot of hokum." Nevertheless, from the 1930s on the distinctiveness of the prehistoric culture of the Arizona desert was recognized.

For the next three decades, Hohokam archaeology again received far less attention than it deserved. Only a few important investigations were carried out, including studies of the Hodges Site in Tucson by Isabel T. Kelly in 1936–38; Pueblo Grande in Phoenix by Albert H. Schroeder in 1938–40; the University Indian Ruin near Tucson by Julian Hayden in 1940; and one of the first multidisciplinary archaeological projects in the United States, Haury's excavation of Ventana Cave on the Papago reservation in 1941–42. But overall, the Great Depression greatly slowed archaeological research in the Southwest, and World War II then diverted archaeologists to other activities.

The extent of contributions to Hohokam culture from the south, whether by a migrating group that settled at Snaketown or through trade contacts, continued to be argued. Neither had it been well established when Hohokam irrigation began—at the start of the Pioneer period (perhaps as early as 300 B.C.) or much later. The relationship of the Hohokam to the Mogollon culture to the east was also argued. And disagreements about chronology continued. David Doyel, former director of the Pueblo Grande Museum in Phoenix, commented, "By the 1960s Hohokam prehistory appeared to be in disarray. The cultural affiliation of the elusive Pioneer period had been ascribed to the Hohokam, Mogollon, O'otam, and Hakataya; Hohokam origins were seen as being local and as a migration from Mexico; and at least three major versions of the chronology existed." As late as 1982 Randall H. McGuire, then completing his Ph.D. at the University of Arizona, could write, "There is mass confusion in Hohokam archaeology with personalities playing a bigger role than objective evaluation of data."

Albert H. Schroeder in the late 1930s. Courtesy Pueblo Grande Museum.

HAURY AND SNAKETOWN REVISITED

Haury had observed, "This chaotic state of affairs convinced me that the only way to solve the dilemma was by launching new studies, that the only reasonable way to argue points under contention was with the shovel." Accordingly, he undertook a new excavation program at Snaketown in 1964–65 with the benefit of field techniques developed since the 1930s, including the use of heavy excavating machinery where appropriate. New dating methods were available, such as carbon-14, archaeomagnetism, alpha-recoil tracks, and obsidian hydration, although

Snaketown excavations, 1964. Courtesy Arizona State Museum, photograph by Helga Teiwes.

the interpretation of the dates continued to be controversial. For example, charcoal from cooking fires might have come from dead wood lying in the desert for many decades, making carbon-14 dates from it misleading. Haury secured much additional information on irrigation canals, although others still disagreed with his date of about 300 B.C. for the beginning of irrigation. Many more house floors were cleared and wells and roasting pits were excavated. Altogether, the results of the second excavation program at Snaketown added immensely to Hohokam archaeology. The intense interest of the Pima Indians, on whose land the site lies, was indicated by the celebratory party the workmen and their families gave for Haury and his archaeological staff at the completion of the field work.

Yet only two years after Haury's report on this new research was published in 1976, he could say, "Hohokam studies in 1978 are about where Anasazi investigations were in 1940." Clearly, something more than its lagging start made the study of Hohokam archaeology so complex and controversial. Part of the difficulty may lie in the length of time elapsed since the occupation of the last Hohokam sites. Even if the Pimas and Papagos were Hohokam descendants, the clear continuity from the prehistoric to the modern used to elucidate Pueblo archaeology did not exist. The study of Hohokam villages was complicated by their dispersed "rancheria" pattern, in contrast to the compact pattern of Pueblo villages. Different views of the areas occupied by the Hohokam were also presented. Haury's earlier distinction between the Hohokam on the Salt and Gila rivers, with large irrigation canals, and Hohokam adapted to the desert area without permanent streams proved to be too simple a dichotomy. One answer to these ideas has been to regard the Hohokam not as a "people" or a "culture" but "a dynamic regional system of interaction" with great regional diversity as well as many common elements. In this model, changes in the Hohokam culture included rapid population growth, increasing complexity in the social system, and shifting of the center of settlement from the Gila to the Salt.

RECENT HOHOKAM STUDIES

Much new information on the Hohokam has been appearing in the last two decades. David Doyel has summarized over sixty major projects conducted between 1973 and 1983, many the result of extensive excavation in advance of highway and other construction projects. For example, freeway building through Phoenix was preceded by studies of several large prehistoric villages that had been poorly known before. Other work has added greatly to knowledge of Pioneer-period houses and their dating. The building of the Central Arizona Project, with its large aqueducts to bring water from the Colorado River to southern Arizona, required archaeological research in many little-known areas that had been considered too marginal to merit serious attention. Much of this work generated a new awareness of "outlying" farming areas and the relationships of seasonal settlements to the densely populated major sites. It also increased our understanding of the flexibility and variety of the ways in which the Hohokam subsisted. Farming methods ranged from irrigation by means of large canals to floodwater farming and dry

Excavation of a ceramic animal cache at the Pueblo Grande ruins by Soil Systems, Inc., prior to construction of a freeway through the site. Courtesy Phoenix Arts Commission, photograph by David Noble,1990.

farming, and they also used a wide range of wild plants.

Recently, exchange and interaction among Hohokam communities have received increasing attention. Trade in plant products and many kinds of manufactured goods was probably more important than previously thought. The reconstruction of past environments is advancing as are settlement-pattern studies. There seem to have been consistent relationships in the spacing of major towns and their relationships to canals: a town was located about 3 miles from a canal intake and others were spaced about 3 miles apart along the canal. The implications of this patterning and of the exceptions to it make another intriguing problem in Hohokam research.

As in all archaeological research, new information stimulates new interpretations and additional data are necessary before those interpretations can be confirmed or denied. At the same time, new ways of looking at information from earlier work advance our understanding of the past. For example, David Wilcox of the Museum of Northern Arizona has used Haury's new information on Snaketown to interpret the pattern of house floors, ball courts, and open areas in terms of the internal social structure of the town, identifying "house clusters" and "courtyards" and proposing that through the years, Hohokam society changed from an egalitarian to a hierarchical system.

The years ahead will undoubtedly bring new and unforeseeable interpretations of Hohokam archaeology, all of which will be argued vigorously. Some will be discarded, some accepted. There is no likelihood that all the questions will be answered or the need for digging will end. While the basic outlines of their remarkable achievements in the desert are becoming ever clearer, the Hohokam will continue to puzzle and amaze.

The study of Hohokam archaeology is not only a search for understanding past events and people, but also a potential means of better understanding our present-day problems. The Hohokam people were successful for many centuries in surviving on the limited resources of the desert, using its few rivers to irrigate their fields, farming dry uplands, harvesting wild products, and adapting their way of life to the area's limitations. We cannot yet say whether their decline was the result of damage to farmland by over-irrigation, allowing salts to build up by evaporation; the growth of population beyond what their natural resources could support; conflicts among towns and villages or hostilities with other groups; the spread of disease through increasingly crowded communities; or catastrophes we have not yet discovered. Today, the desert has a vastly greater population than in prehistoric times, but the desert does not support this population as it did in the past. It may be several decades before it will be clear whether our present, very different pattern of desert occupation can be as successful as that of the ancient Hohokam. Meanwhile, what we can learn about the balance the Hohokam achieved between natural resources and the demands of their way of life may help assure us a more successful future in our use of the environment we depend on.

Craft Arts of the Hohokam

Patricia L. Crown

T HE SONORAN DESERT curates a legacy from the past. An insistent sun rapidly evaporates the scant rainfall and preserves this legacy in dry heat. In this still expanse, tools and ornaments fashioned by long-deceased artisans lie in the homes, courtyards, and trash heaps where they were abandoned by their owners. Over the centuries, the caliche, adobe, and wood homes have melted back into the desert, leaving few traces of once bustling communities. Perhaps by design, Hohokam communities blend into their surroundings in a way that Anasazi stone masonry sites do not. Trained archaeologists squint against the desert glare, finding houses and features hard to discern in a landscape washed by the sun's reflection. And in what is jokingly referred to as "braille" archaeology, often only the ring of a trowel, a slightly flaky texture, or more resistant soil alert archaeologists to the adobe or caliche walls of Hohokam houses.

Domestic architecture met the needs of everyday existence with little elaboration, but Hohokam crafts reveal a quality of workmanship and love of beauty that contrasts with the austere homes in which they were used or worn. The Hohokam were highly skilled crafts producers and traded widely for artifacts

Ceramic figurines excavated from Snaketown. Courtesy Arizona State Museum, photograph by Helga Teiwes.

Display of outstanding Hohokam ceramics dating ca. A.D. 800 to1100. Courtesy Arizona State Museum, photograph by Helga Teiwes.

produced in other portions of the Southwest. Often, these materials are more instrumental to archaeologists in finding a community and determining what went on there than is the chameleon-like architecture.

THE ARTISANS

The Hohokam fashioned ornamental and utilitarian objects of clay, stone, bone, shell, wood, and fiber. Because shell and some kinds of stone were not available in the desert, they were brought by traders to the Hohokam area from as far away as the Gulf of Mexico. Hohokam pottery found on the beach near Los Angeles attests to the distant trading relations maintained by these resourceful artisans.

Most crafts were utilitarian and probably produced by family members for their own use, but individuals of great ability must have crafted some rare items that required deftness beyond the norm. Archaeologists believe that some kinds of pottery, some stone tools, and shell ornaments were crafted by artisans working part-time to supply whole communities. Some of these specialists strove to perfect their craft; ornamental projectile points reveal the dexterity attained by only a few specialists. But for others, speed and quantity replaced quality as a goal, and their crafts were obviously made and decorated with less care.

THE CRAFTS

Pottery and potsherds far surpass in quantity any other artifacts found at Hohokam village sites. The earliest pottery vessels appeared some time before A.D. 200, the idea of pottery manufacture drifting northward from Mexico into the Hohokam desert. Prehistoric potters gathered clays from various sources on the desert floor and in adjacent mountain ranges and collected sand and micaceous schist to mix with the clay as temper to prevent shrinkage and cracking during drying and firing.

Early vessels were modeled in one of two ways. Potters built some pots of thin snakes of clay, coiling the clay ropes into various container forms and thinning their walls by scraping them with a smooth piece of pottery, gourd, or stone. They built other pots in fat coils, thinning the walls by patting the exterior with a wooden paddle (shaped like a small pizza paddle) while the interior was supported by a mushroom-shaped stone anvil. The mushroom shape made this anvil easy to hold against the moist clay walls. Through time, the paddle-and-anvil technique replaced the coil-and-scrape technique as the preferred method for pottery production among the Hohokam. Potters worked their mixture of clay, rock temper, and water into jars, cauldrons, censers, plates, bowls, ladles, effigies, and figurines. They then stacked the vessels in shallow pits, covered them with large sherds to protect them from the fuel, and fired them using mesquite wood in an atmosphere with free access to oxygen. The completed pots ranged in color from a clear buff to a deep brown.

Most vessels were not decorated, but some were covered with a red slip and polished, and others were painted with red designs. In early times, potters incised lines in the exterior of some bowls, with a tool, deepening the grooves between the

Santa Cruz Red-on-buff ceramics. Courtesy Arizona State Museum, photograph by Helga Teiwes.

rope-like coils. Later potters occasionally traced ornamental coils on the smoothed bowl walls, leaving shallow, irregular furrows. The earliest painted designs consisted of thick lines, probably finger-applied, in chevrons or crude spirals. The background color was an unslipped gray mottled with "fire-clouds," created when vessel walls and fuel came into contact.

Through time, Hohokam potters gained greater control over their firing atmosphere and their materials, lightening the background color to a consistent buff and painting finer lines. By A.D. 600, decorations consisted almost entirely of large geometric shapes filled with hatches so finely painted that they often yield a solid effect. After A.D. 700, potters began filling vessel walls with repetitive geometric designs, that is, small geometric shapes painted over and over in tightly packed spaces. Some geometric shapes occur so often that they have come to be known as the "Hohokam alphabet," although there is no evidence that they constituted any form of written language. The effect of hundreds of small shapes in red paint against a clean

Sacaton Red-on-buff vessels. Courtesy Arizona State Museum, photograph by Helga Teiwes.

buff background is mesmerizing. The designs are impeccably executed, intricate line work evenly spaced across the vessel walls. The quality of the craft reached an apex by A.D. 900, only to decline as demands for quantity replaced the delicate artistry of earlier times. Between A.D. 900 and 1100, potters tended to paint large vessels with large geometric shapes. Although these late vessels are appealing, the emphasis had clearly changed.

By about A.D. 1200, aspects of the distinctive Hohokam style died out. Red-on-buff pottery production declined, replaced largely by polychrome pottery quite different from the earlier vessels, indicating major technological and stylistic change. Potters manufactured many more red-slipped vessels, using innovative techniques. Polishing striations produced with stone tools yielded lustrous patterns in the finished red vessels, and large teardrop-shaped fire-clouds were smoked permanently into the vessel wall by artful placement of fuel. The Hohokam moved from their dispersed pithouse residences to pueblo-like adobe compounds, and some people occupied homes on top of massive

Child's cotton poncho from Ventana Cave. Courtesy Arizona State Museum, photograph by E. B. Sayles.

Etched shell. Courtesy Arizona State Museum, photograph by E. B. Sayles.

platform mounds reflecting greater social stratification. Large sites of this time over a broad portion of the Southwest produce not only polychrome pottery, but also a common set of ornaments, such as turquoise-encrusted shell frogs.

Regardless of how fine their craftsmanship, Hohokam vessels show evidence of use. Miniature vessels may be children's toys, and some of the clumsily molded, awkwardly painted vessels may have been the first efforts of budding artisans. Larger Hohokam pottery was used throughout the life of the owner for cooking, carrying water, storing food and water, serving, eating, ladling, and probably in rituals. Thick-walled "censers" may have held burning incense for ritual performances or some other religious use. Ladles have asymmetric, ground edges documenting whether the owner was right or left handed. Pottery often accompanied the Hohokam into death, and after A.D. 900 their cremated bones were buried in jars and covered with inverted bowls.

Clay was also fashioned into human and animal figurines. Although the figurines can be interpreted as children's toys, their occurrence in cremations and caches suggests otherwise. Caching of deer figurines may have played a role in rituals intended to increase the animals' fertility or improve the hunters' skill. The human figurines are particularly intriguing, suggesting that the Hohokam dressed scantily, wore their hair wrapped with headbands or turbans, decorated their faces with earrings and cheek plugs, and ornamented their bodies with paint and tattoos.

Few Hohokam textiles survive, but the few available indicate great skill in weaving. Weavers created blankets, kilts, breech clouts, and sleeveless shirts for protection against the elements and personal adornment. Caches of ceremonial cane cigarettes, each wrapped in a miniature cotton sash, have been found in caves in the Hohokam area. The benign desert environment permitted the Hohokam to grow cotton, and they may have supplied raw cotton and finished textiles to other portions of the Southwest.

The Hohokam excelled also in the production of groundstone artifacts, particularly palettes and stone bowls, but they were probably best known for the manufacture of shell ornaments. Shell from the Pacific Coast and the Gulf of California is scattered throughout Hohokam sites, and debris attests to the transformation of much of the material from raw shell to finished product at Hohokam sites. Craft producers worked shell into beads, pendants, bracelets, rings, sculpted geometric shapes, and trumpets. Shell was further modified by drilling, carving, painting or etching. The care taken in working shell is exemplified by holes in beads of such small size and uniform diameter that it is believed they were drilled using cactus spines and a fine abrasive, such as a sand grain. Etching may represent the pinnacle of shell-working art. An organic resist was applied to the shell, protecting a portion of the surface. The shell was then dipped in an acidic solution, perhaps the fermented juice of the saguaro cactus, which ate away the uncoated portions of the shell surface. Removal of the resist left a delicate, raised surface design. Shell ornaments manufactured by Hohokam artisans or manufactured to the south and exchanged through Hohokam traders are also found in Anasazi and Mogollon sites to the north and east.

LIFEFORMS

The Sonoran desert appears barren to us today, but before the damming of the rivers, it teemed with life. In stone, ceramics, bone, and shell, the Hohokam portrayed living creatures with a skill unmatched in the prehistoric Southwest. Lifeforms occur elsewhere, but seldom with the powerful sense of motion and energy depicted by the Hohokam. Snakes slither, lizards wriggle, turtles creep, birds float, scorpions scrabble, and fish swim across the curving surfaces of Hohokam pottery, shell, and stone bowls. Although stylized, the species are unmistakable, dynamic, and oddly benign. Even in scenes of long-billed water birds attacking coiling snakes, the images are cartoon-like, even charming, and certainly devoid of any sinister feel. Lifeforms were painted on pottery with a minimum of brush strokes, resulting in a whimsical appearance. Although we may be biased by Western aesthetics,

Above: Carved bone effigy of a mountain sheep. Left: Stone horned lizard. Courtesy Arizona State Museum, photographs by Helga Teiwes.

it is easy to view these images as a strong commentary on the Hohokam character. Affection for and amusement with animals emerges from their art. Attuned to life in the desert, they were masters of their environment, not daunted by it.

Generally, humans were also painted in motion: dancing, playing the flute, carrying burden baskets and canes, hunting with bow and arrow. They carry rattles, wear feather headdresses, hold hands. The human effigy jars depict benevolent, Buddha-like figures with enormous bodies, spindly limbs, protruding noses and ears, and coffee-bean eyes. Are these caricatures of specific individuals, self portraits, or representations of supernatural beings? Unfortunately, the answer lies in a time and with people we cannot ask.

For the Anasazi and Mogollon, the two other major cultures in the Southwest, controlling the climate through rituals was important for survival. Frost and drought were ever-present threats to growing crops. Irrigation farming gave the Hohokam greater control over their environment. Devastating floods might destroy the canal network, but climatic events had not nearly the import that they did for their neighbors without ditches. Instead, coordination in water allocation and maintenance of the ditches encouraged cooperation among all families sharing a single ditch. Perhaps this need for cooperation underlies the frequent portrayal of humans encircling pottery, holding hands in lines with no beginning and no end.

In their crafts, the Hohokam left us a legacy that tells us much that archaeological sites alone cannot. The beneficent environment promoted the cultural stability reflected in these crafts. It also permitted at least part-time specialization in craft production. Increasing control over materials and techniques accompanies gradual change in crafts until A.D. 1200, but the solidity of the technological tradition provided a foundation for the decorative creativity and skill apparent in the artwork. The Hohokam clearly prized imaginative renderings and appreciated the beauty of their desert landscape. Even so, as shown in depictions of birds attacking snakes, they recognized that conflict and death were a part of its natural order.

Above: Quails decorate a ceramic plate.
Below: Ceramic Buddha-like figure.
Courtesy Arizona State Museum,
photographs by Helga Teiwes.

Hohokam Religion

An Archaeologist's Perspective

David R. Wilcox

I FIRST BEGAN WONDERING about Hohokam religion while studying Hohokam ball courts. These large, oval depressions are surrounded by earthen embankments and occur in two size classes, one about 82 feet long by 49 feet wide, and the other as much as 200 feet long and 108 feet wide. They are clearly some form of public architecture in Hohokam villages. More than two hundred courts in more than 160 sites are now known, all in Arizona, centered in the Phoenix Basin. As David

Partially excavated ball court at Snaketown. Courtesy Arizona State Museum.

A rubber ball (average diameter 2.75 inches) excavated in 1909 from a Hohokam site near Toltec, Arizona. The ball, which dates from between A.D. 900 and 1200, possibly was used in the ritual ball game. Collections of the Southwest Museum. Photograph by Emil Haury, courtesy Arizona State Museum.

Doyel has pointed out in his preceding article, hundreds of people could have stood on the embankments and watched the activities within.

In 1935, Emil Haury first noticed the analogy between Hohokam and Mesoamerican ball courts. Carved stone sculptures, paintings on ceramics, and other data show that the latter were the scene of elaborate ritual "games" in which a solid rubber ball was batted back and forth by two teams using only their hips or arms. A microcosm of the cosmos, the game simulated the movements of the deities in an effort to make the world a liveable place for humans. Perhaps a version of this Mesoamerican ritual was also practiced by the Hohokam.

The implications of Haury's bold idea were far reaching. First, if he were right, the Hohokam would have been closely linked culturally to Mesoamerican societies a thousand or more miles to the south. Second, Hohokam society throughout southern Arizona was apparently tightly integrated by a network of ball courts where public rituals were conducted, graphically displaying both the integration and opposing rivalries of Hohokam social groups.

Once I grasped the possibility of interactions between the Hohokam and Mesoamericans, whose great religious traditions gave legitimacy to complex political systems, I began to focus my research on the relationship between Hohokam social organization and religion. But there was a hitch. In 1967, Edwin Ferdon had argued persuasively that the Hohokam courts were not really ball courts, correctly pointing out that Mesoamerican courts are rectangular with flat playing alleys, whereas the Hohokam courts are oval with slightly sloping floors. If these formal differences are functionally significant, then the Hohokam courts were probably not used as ball courts. Perhaps they were dance plazas, as Ferdon suggested. Should we then forget about Mesoamerican influences on southwestern religions?

Ferdon's is a good argument, but there is an answer to it. If the ball game, but not the ball court itself, were adopted from Mexico, the formal differences in the courts may be the result of independent modification of ball court design in southern Arizona. The important question, then, is whether or not a version of the Mesoamerican ball game could have been played on the Hohokam courts. Their size, symmetry, and smooth surfaces all support this possibility. Consequently, I have started to look for other data on Hohokam religion, its relationships to Mesoamerica, and its evolution. I present here a sketch of my current synthesis.

EARLY HOHOKAM RELIGION

About 1000 B.C., Archaic populations in southern Arizona began raising corn, living in hamlets, and burying their dead in a flexed position within their settlements. These developments all point to the slow emergence of new forms of social organization and ideological belief.

As David Doyel discusses in his chapter of this issue, between A.D. 250 and 550, Snaketown inhabitants built a group of successively occupied extra-large houses centered on a large plaza, which was probably the scene of public dances and rituals. The community headmen, who organized intervillage ceremonial events, may have lived in these special houses.

The earliest ceramic designs found in the Hohokam area consist of broad red lines dividing bowl interiors into four quarters. This design could symbolize the general New World cosmological belief in a universe divided into four quarters.

Another clue to Hohokam religion in the early centuries A.D. is the occurrence of hundreds of clay figurines, a few of which appear to represent ballplayers. Perhaps the early ritual ball game was played in the plaza without formal courts. Bone tubes, some of which are incised, have also been found; they may have been used as sucking tubes by shamans in curing rituals. New beliefs about death and social differentiation are indicated by the cremation of a few individuals and a continuation of the older practice of flexed burial for others.

Beginning about A.D. 550, the Hohokam made significant technological advances such as the bow and arrow and large-scale irrigation systems. Their population increased, and new forms of social organization and religious beliefs emerged. As Henry Wallace discusses in this issue, the Hohokam developed a new style of rock art emphasizing human and animal lifeforms. In ceramic design, birds and lizards were outlined by hachured areas, as were zigzags (possibly symbolizing lightning) and abstract flying birds. The designs seem to have had more than a purely decorative function, and the small repertoire of animals is repeated over and over again. These factors suggest to me that the designs held sacred status and may even have been the icons of deities. The shift to representational art is paralleled in West Mexico; however, local species were portrayed in the Phoenix Basin. Thus, although possibly influenced from the outside, the Hohokam were expressing their own distinctive religious and aesthetic system.

Archaeologists believe that the construction of caliche-capped mounds at Snaketown indicates a new kind of ritual facility. The caching of smashed miniature clay vessels called "censers" would become a long-enduring religious practice. Their interment probably followed a special ceremonial event.

Artist's rendering of Hohokam dancers, ca. A.D. 900. The dancers are wearing cotton skirts and sashes, and necklaces and headbands of imported marine shell. Brightly colored macaw feathers emanate from their headbands. Reconstruction was aided by drawings of Hohokam clay figurines and pottery designs. Drawing by John Joha in collaboration with David E. Doyel.

RELIGIOUS FLORESCENCE
The Hohokam religious system achieved its most elaborate and culturally influential form from A.D. 750 to 1000. The Hohokam constructed a network of large and small ball courts between A.D. 750 and 800 and, at the same time, began to practice an elaborate death ritual involving cremation and ritual paraphernalia (palettes and stone bowls) made out of imported materials such as slate, tuff, and argillite. In the A.D. 800s, they built ball courts in Mogollon territory to the east and north and extended their

religious influence even into the Mimbres area and upper Little Colorado Valley.

What brought about these changes? The new religious ideology correlates with a fundamental reorganization of the production and consumption groups that composed Hohokam society. Before this ideology went into effect, Hohokam houses were grouped around courtyards. For the first time in the A.D. 700s, these courtyard groups began to aggregate into "suprahousehold" groups, the members of which buried their dead in a nearby cemetery. It seems likely that these suprahouseholds were corporate landowning groups who controlled the inheritance of valuable irrigated land and marked their social identities in a series of ceremonies involving the ball game and death rituals.

MESOAMERICAN INFLUENCES

Mesoamerican ideas may have been an important stimulus in these transformations, suggesting ways to legitimize the new social and political relations that were emerging. In West Mexico, I-shaped ball courts are present in the large sites of the Teuchitlan cultural tradition, which dates to the first millennium A.D. And other aspects of this Mesoamerican civilization were present in the Hohokam area just at the time the Hohokam religion was elaborated.

Thomas Holien, a student of West Mexican prehistory, has shown that the Teuchitlan tradition of the lakes district of Jalisco was the cultural heart of a pseudo-cloisonné art style in which artisans expressed a glyph-like iconography on jars and open bowls with high annular pedestals. Holien thinks these objects, which are usually found together in burials, were used in ritual drinking. A secondary center of this art style is in the Chalchihuites area of Zacatecas, northeast of Jalisco. In both areas, sandstone discs with iron pyrites glued to one side and pseudo-cloisonné designs on the other have been found in association with high-status burials. Holien interprets these associations as evidence of deity impersonation (a priest dressing in the guise of a god and sometimes becoming one with the deity) and ritual immolation.

Iron-pyrite "mirror" discs, some with pseudo-cloisonné designs, have been found in several Hohokam sites, both in

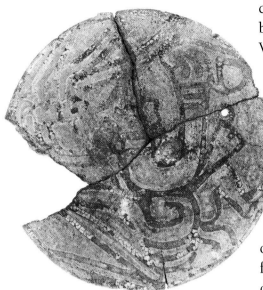

Long-nosed glyph on mirror back from Grewe Site. Courtesy Natural History Museum of Los Angeles County.

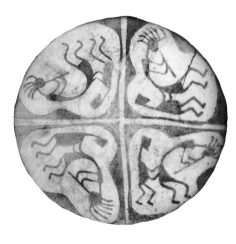

Ceramic bowl depicting flute players wearing feathers. Courtesy Arizona State Museum, photograph by Helga Teiwes.

cremations and in caches without cremated bone. The discs date between A.D. 700 and 900, and Holien believes they derive from West Mexico, either the Teuchitlan or the Chalchihuites area. They first occur in the Hohokam area just at the time that cremation death ritual was elaborated.

Arthur Woodward found the most dramatic specimen of this kind at the Grewe Site on the Gila River near Casa Grande Ruins in 1930. It portrays a glyph of a long-nosed god or deity impersonator. Four feather-like plumes project from an elaborate headdress. The feet are in a dance-like posture, and the figure is moving forward, to the right. An exaggerated right arm reaches forward, holding an unidentified object. On the right hand is a glove with three large claws. The figure also wears a sash (below the arm) and a bustle-like object on its waist. The presence of this glyph shows that the Hohokam came face to face with the iconography of a high civilization.

How did this come about? Although we are still unsure, we can suggest several hypotheses. Basic to all of them is that Piman, the language spoken in southern Arizona in the historic period, was only dialectically different from Tepehuan, which was spoken in Durango and Zacatecas. Linguists call the common language Tepiman. We have no reason to doubt that a chain of dialects forming a communication corridor from the Hohokam area to the Chalchihuites area existed prehistorically.

When elaborate new ceremonial facilities were built at Alta Vista in Zacatecas in the A.D. 700s or 800s, news of the religious excitement this generated could have been carried quickly to the Hohokam by people coming north. Alternatively, Hohokam novices may have traveled south to study at Alta Vista or other West Mexico religious centers, returning with tokens of their trip in the form of iron-pyrite mirrors. Seeing these objects, who at that time would have dared to challenge the legitimacy of their owners or their power to direct Hohokam religious activities?

Possibilities that cast doubt on the claim of Mesoamerican influence must also be considered. A bird with a curved beak is shown on another mirror back from the Grewe Site. It may be a parrot. Many birds are portrayed in Hohokam iconography from this time, usually quail and local water birds such as herons or pelicans. However, parrot-like designs are exceedingly rare. Lizards (probably the horned toad), turtles, and snakes also are common. Humans are shown in several ways, often as lines of identical dancing figures holding hands. Burden carriers holding a crooked stick and flute players wearing feathers in their hair are also pictured. There is nothing particularly Mesoamerican about any of this; if Mesoamerican ideas did affect the Hohokam, they must have been reinterpreted in local terms.

The lizard icon appears to have had considerable importance. It is the only one pictured in all media: ceramics, slate palettes, carved shell and stone bowls, and rock art. A bowl sherd found at Snaketown shows a large lizard figure surrounded by dancers circling it in a counterclockwise motion. From the last part of the Hohokam period, the anthropomorph on an effigy jar wears a lizard figure around its neck, perhaps a sign of office. Similar anthropomorphic jars are known from the Anasazi area, but without lizards. Did the Hohokam have a lizard deity?

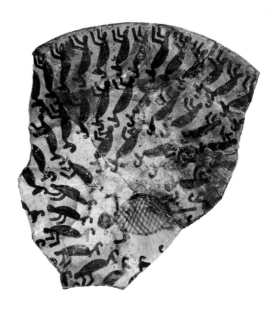

Above: Potsherd depicting lizard surrounded by dancers. Left: Anthropomorphic effigy vessel with lizard on necklace. Courtesy Arizona State Museum, photographs by Helga Teiwes.

Stone palettes from Snaketown. Courtesy Arizona State Museum, photograph by Helga Teiwes.

CENSERS, PALETTES, AND FIGURINES

Archaeologists have found caches of broken or burned stone bowls in both the Phoenix and Tucson basins. The bowls are usually made of argillite, tuff, vesicular basalt, or some other imported material. In several cases, a phallus projects from the bowl, while in other cases, a snake occupies a similar position.

Although they have been called "censers," no evidence has been found to indicate that incense was burned either in these small stone bowls or in later, ceramic, thick-walled bowls. They more likely held a small amount of liquid that was a symbol of

54 • DAVID R. WILCOX

potency—possibly human blood. In an interesting argument, Gary Feinman has suggested that scarifiers were present in the Southwest, just as in Mesoamerica, and that they were used to draw blood for sacrificial purposes. Pointed rod-like stones and bone awls previously regarded as "hairpins" both may have had this purpose.

Another characteristic Hohokam artifact, often found in cremations, is the stone palette. Red hematite has been found on some of them, and many bear a lead oxide crust on the surface. When lead is heated, it turns from silver-white to red, and this transformation may have had religious meaning to the Hohokam. Also, clay figurines and ceramic designs show that the Hohokam used body paint, suggesting that hematite and lead were powdered to make paint.

By about A.D. 800, clay figurines were being made less frequently than they had been, but the discoveries of several caches of them associated with cremations in the Phoenix and Tucson basins provide us with an incredibly detailed picture of the death ritual. In one cache, twenty-one figurines were found, including five to seven males and thirteen females (two pregnant), and in another, twenty-six figurines, including six standing males and ten females, eight seated females, one infant, one kneeling male, and parts of four males and one female. Many of the males wear three-strand necklaces, and many of the females have red stripes painted on their abdomens. The male figurines are much larger than most of the females, some of which may actually represent children. Also discovered in these caches were miniature vessels, miniature mano-and-metate sets, and models of *ramadas* with items, possibly food, piled under them. A third cache from the Tucson area contained large figurines of male flute players that had once had feathers in their hair, indicated by the ceramic designs.

How should we interpret these remarkable figurine caches? If size differences relate to age differences, then they may represent the suprahousehold kin groups that attended the funeral. Corn was probably ground and flutes played as part of the ceremony. People may also have brought food, pottery, and other goods. The figurines then accompanied the dead to their resting place in the underworld.

Stone censer from Snaketown. Courtesy Arizona State Museum, photograph by Helga Teiwes.

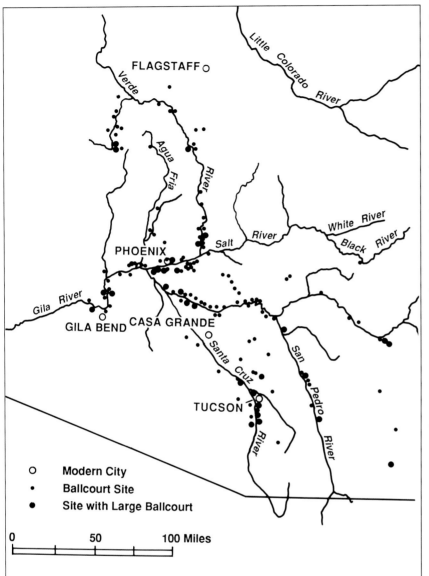

Distribution of Hohokam ball courts.
Map by Katrina Lasko.

Map legend:
- ○ Modern City
- • Ballcourt Site
- ⬤ Site with Large Ballcourt

0   50   100 Miles

A SHRINKING REGIONAL SYSTEM

After A.D. 1000, the Hohokam regional system began to shrink, and a major social and political reorganization began. New ideologies centered in the Mimbres Valley, the Tucson Basin, and the Prescott-Verde Valley area. In addition, the residents of Chaco Canyon began to compete with the Hohokam for the allegiance of intervening people. Networks of exchange were restructured. In the Phoenix Basin, the Salt River Valley superseded the Gila as the primary population center, and its villages took over control of the ball court network, which, by A.D. 1150, had extended as far north as Wupatki, near Flagstaff.

The Hohokam in the Phoenix Basin continued to create their traditional religious symbols. Ceramic design became more complex and abstract, usually involving the juxtaposition or interweaving of two different motifs, perhaps symbolizing the integration of a dual organization. Such "moiety" systems are widespread in the New World. The Eastern Pueblos, for example, have such a system, and in the eleventh century the Hohokam may have adopted this more complex form of social organization. The fact that hand-holding human figures are now portrayed differently from one another suggests that the ceremonies had now come to integrate functionally differentiated roles.

At Snaketown, the Hohokam built eight artificial mounds around the central plaza. This ring of ceremonial facilities was flanked by a large east-west ball court on the west and a small north-south ball court on the east. Along a line between the courts, next to the plaza, two extra-large houses faced one another. They may have been council or moiety houses. The

numerous discrete ceramic designs from this period may be clan symbols. Taken as a whole, the evidence available suggests increasing social integration in which the religion became more complex. The Eastern Pueblos provide an interesting analogue of what form these changes may have taken.

Diverse dancing figures on Sacaton Red-on-buff bowl. Courtesy Arizona State Museum, photograph by Helga Teiwes.

CRISES AND CHANGE

A crisis occurred in Hohokam society sometime around A.D. 1100. Snaketown and certain other sites were abandoned, and a new pattern of three discrete site clusters or polities appeared. By the late A.D. 1200s, the Salt River Valley polity may have controlled the other two.

The nature of death ritual also changed radically about A.D. 1100. Palettes, stone bowls, ceramic "censers," and the lizard-snake-quail-water bird symbols all abruptly disappeared. New symbols, which may be the icons of different deities, now became dominant: the toad (or frog) and raptorial bird. Platform mounds surrounded by palisades, which had first appeared in the previous period, now became centrally important and were periodically enlarged. The leaders of priesthoods or secular war leaders and their households lived near them in distinct ritual precincts outside the palisades. Nose and lip plugs made of argillite or other exotic materials like those worn in the Flagstaff area were imported and worn to display important status. In rock art, a peculiar symbol (called a "pipette" by Henry Wallace) was introduced—perhaps a representation of Tlaloc, the Mesoamerican deity.

Sometime in the mid A.D. 1200s, the elite residences were relocated on top of the mounds, and a large, rectangular compound wall was placed around them. The largest of these walls enclosed an area of over 13,000 square meters. Ball courts were apparently abandoned by about A.D. 1200. After A.D. 1300, multistory towers such as the four-story Casa Grande were built, apparently as astronomical observatories. The elite priests may have used astronomical knowledge to control the calendar and hence the schedule of ceremonial events, thus mediating between their people and the deities.

The toad and raptorial bird symbols were portrayed in elaborate turquoise, argillite, and shell mosaics. These rare and expensive symbols were worn as pendants by very few people, and they were buried with the dead, including infants. The Hohokam may have worn these objects as symbols of leadership in important cults.

Interestingly, the same turquoise-mosaic symbols are found throughout southern Arizona from the Flagstaff area to Casas Grandes, in northwestern Chihuahua. They are slightly more widely distributed than Salado Polychrome pottery, depicting rattlesnake and parrot icons, which were of great importance at Casas Grandes. The elite of the Phoenix Basin polities thus participated in religious and status systems extending well beyond their territory. Its symbols and rituals were quite different from those of the old-time Hohokam religion.

Burial practices at this time were also diverse. As in the Pueblo area, infants or young children were often buried under house floors. On the platform mounds, elite adults were buried fully extended on their backs, with their heads to the east. Other extended burials occur both inside and outside compounds. Most compounds (except those with platform mounds) have cremation cemeteries nearby. Salado polychromes were buried with a select few inhumations and cremations and with burials both on and off platform mounds. The complexity of the social and political system is apparent in this diversity of burial treatment.

Between A.D. 1356 and 1382, heavy winter flows in the Salt and Gila rivers may have had catastrophic effects on the Hohokam canal systems. Other evidence suggests that the civic authority of the platform-mound elites was destroyed, and it seems likely that profound changes in religious systems also occurred. Abandonment soon followed. By 1694, when we next have data to work with, Piman-speaking people lived in the Gila Valley, and the lower Salt was a wilderness.

We can conclude from this sketch of the evolution of Hohokam religion and its relationship to social and political organization that it was far from static. On the contrary, at least two revolutions of religious belief are apparent. The first happened in the A.D. 700s, when a combination of Mesoamerican and local ideas were synthesized to form the first distinctively "Hohokam" religion. During the first century of its existence, this ideology provoked considerable interest from neighboring populations, but beginning in about A.D. 1000, as the Hohokam in the Phoenix Basin created a more elaborate and complex version of it, its general influence waned. The second revolution came around A.D. 1100, when radical settlement changes came about and the vertical differentiation of decision-making authority within the society increased. Elite priests, who controlled religious knowledge, now began to intervene between the common folk and the deities, perhaps legitimizing their power by associating themselves with the gods. The religious community thus politically integrated in the Phoenix Basin may have included as many as thirty thousand people at its height. But then catastrophe struck when, in the mid-1300s, two disastrous Salt River floods are thought to have destroyed the canal systems of the Hohokam. The enormous fluctuations of a desert environment thus finally caught up with human pretensions to omnipotence.

Pictures in the Desert

Hohokam Rock Art

Henry D. Wallace

*T*HROUGHOUT much of southern Arizona, scattered on low, rocky buttes and marking long-forgotten trails, images drawn on rocks by the prehistoric Hohokam Indians can be found. These drawings occur at hundreds of sites within the range of the Hohokam. The most common are petroglyphs, which are pecked or scratched into the rock surface; only a handful of sites with pictographs, or painted designs, are known. Together with the colorful pottery that defines Hohokam culture, rock art provides a graphic insight into the thought and expression of this ancient people.

HOHOKAM ORIGINS AND ROCK ART

The artistic expression we see in Hohokam rock art has its roots in the designs of the much older Western Archaic tradition. This more ancient pictography was created by seminomadic hunters, gatherers, and horticulturists who ranged through what is now the western United States and northern Mexico between around 7500 B.C. and A.D. 450. Western Archaic abstract rock art conveys a cultural philosophy or world view shared by many peoples throughout this large region. In southern Arizona, the evident continuity of style from Western Archaic to Hohokam suggests that the Hohokam Indians did not immigrate from Mexico, as once believed, but rather had their origins among local indigenous folk.

The striking pipette figure, thought to be unique to Hohokam rock art. Photograph by Henry Wallace.

Characteristic Hohokam petroglyph panel in the Phoenix Basin. Photograph by David Noble, 1990.

Hohokam rock art shares certain key design traits with Hohokam pottery of specific periods. For example, the single largest shift in Hohokam pottery style occurred near the end of the Pioneer period (A.D. 450-750) when abstract designs resembling Western Archaic style gave way to a wealth of new geometric shapes and life-forms, including animals, birds, reptiles, insects, and humans. At the same time, rock "artists" added similar naturalistic motifs to their existing abstract style and modified traditional abstract designs. This mix of continuity and change in rock art style reinforces recent archaeological findings that place the beginnings of Hohokam culture in the same time frame.

Another important measure of time lies in patina dating, with which scientists analyze the brown or blackish coating on rock surfaces, the product of gradual chemical and mechanical changes over time. In this formation process, wind-deposited particles of clay adhering to the rock surface provide a toehold for a bacterial microorganism that actually converts the minerals in the accumulated clay into a thin, rock-hard, metallic varnish composed largely of manganese and iron. By pecking or scratching through the patina to reveal the lighter rock interior, the newly exposed surface would then gradually develop its own patina and darken. In some cases, it is possible to assess the relative ages of petroglyphs by comparing the effects of these processes.

The representational imagery distinguishing the Hohokam style from that of the Western Archaic includes sheep, deer, dogs or coyotes, snakes, lizards, tortoises, and possibly antelope. Most common are sheep and deer, sometimes shown with oversized horns or antlers. Occasionally sheep are drawn with their horns reversed or with one horn forward and one backwards. Birds are rare in Hohokam imagery but one can find egrets or herons, pelicans, and "thunderbirds." Insect-like images, also rare, include what appear to be ticks or mites and dragonflies.

Hohokam rock art differs in both motifs and style from that

Typical abstract designs. Photograph by Henry Wallace.

found in the more familiar rock art galleries of northern Arizona, New Mexico, and southern Utah. Simple Hohokam anthropomorphic stick figures, often with small, circular midsections, for example, contrast to the full filled-in bodies typical of Anasazi petroglyphs. Also, Hohokam figures often have three fingers and toes. Occasional panels bear distinctive human figures with hourglass bodies, a trademark of Hohokam pottery design.

A multitude of geometric abstract forms accompany the representational figures. Very likely, many common images that seem undecipherably abstract to modern viewers—simple, concentric, and rayed circles; meandering lines; "bull's eyes"; "asterisks"; and "barbells"—represented familiar concepts to the Hohokam. Patterned arrangements called "dint patterns" and a ghostly figure called a "pipette" tend to occur only at the largest sites. In some cases, many different abstract designs are pecked together, forming a large, complex, and often spectacular panel.

The only easily recognizable man-made items in Hohokam rock art are bows and arrows, staffs, and flutes. A flute player is occasionally seen, perhaps representing Kokopelli, the familiar humpbacked flute player of Pueblo mythology and rock art. Other anthropomorphic figures sometimes wear elaborate headdresses or

Human figure with expanded midbody. Photograph by Henry Wallace.

Hohokam petroglyph depicting a dance ceremony. Photograph by David Noble, 1990.

hair ornaments and various additions to their bodies, perhaps signifying special or ceremonial clothing.

Most naturalistic Hohokam images tend to be static, one design rarely being linked to others in a dynamic way. There are, however, exceptions to this general rule, including occasional lines of dancers, apparent hunting scenes, and other narrative groups of images. Overall, the images in Hohokam petroglyph panels give the impression of being haphazardly arranged. Panels that do provide clear insight, therefore, are treasured windows into prehistory.

INTERPRETING ROCK ART

What does Hohokam rock art mean? For all our efforts to comprehend these fascinating images, their significance remains elusive. And yet, some educated guesses are possible. Three broad themes that we can recognize throughout the imagery are hunting, ritual, and fertility. In presumed hunting scenes, we find human figures, bows and arrows, and prey animals in various combinations. Sheep sometimes are illustrated upside down, possibly indicating their death, accompanied by a person with arms upraised. We can only guess what such scenes meant to the Hohokam: a successful past hunt, a request for future good hunting, or something entirely different.

Panels depicting shamanic figures with what seem to be body ornaments and ritual paraphernalia certainly suggest religious activity. In one such case, a shaman holding something in his mouth stands over a small, prostrate figure, while a third person dances nearby. Could this be a curing ceremony? Another recurring scene in which we recognize ritual characteristics is a line of dancers holding hands. Still another, which seems to show a human birth, includes what we might interpret as a mother, infant, umbilical cord, and placenta.

One petroglyph that we surmise held special meaning to the Hohokam is the pipette, an abstract image that usually appears prominently, but which is sometimes concealed at larger rock art sites. The pipette, with its set of connected and stacked rectangular tiers and two eye-like circles, gives a ghostly effect to certain panels. The special attributes of this striking design bring to mind certain Jornada rock art images in southern New Mexico, which probably portray Tlaloc, a Mesoamerican rain god characterized by distinctive goggle eyes. Might the pipettes in the Hohokam area represent a similar deity?

Some Hohokam petroglyphs apparently represent surrounding landscape features. A glyph in the Picacho Mountains, for example, seems to trace the outline of the ridge on which it is located. Another, on display at the Kitt Peak Observatory near Tucson, bears an apparent plan view of a house cluster. If this interpretation is accurate, it shows that the Hohokam, like modern archaeologists, perceived house clusters as social units.

Where do we find Hohokam petroglyphs? And can we tell what the Indians were doing at these sites, other than drawing on the rocks? Scholars studying the environmental and cultural associations of Hohokam rock art have found glyph concentrations at springs and along streams, at stone quarries, along prehistoric trails, and where the Hohokam were processing wild plants for food.

Archaeologists have long been skeptical of rock art studies because of problems of direct interpretation. But some recent research clearly demonstrates the potential to delve into aspects of culture that cannot be probed through traditional archaeological methods. Investigations at some small rock shelters at a petroglyph site in the Picacho Mountains, for example, revealed that the shelters were the scene of ritual activities.

Above: Possible hunting scene with a symbolically killed sheep, a hunter, and another figure. Below: Possible birth scene. Photographs by Henry Wallace.

During seismic activity, the upper boulder bounced into the lower boulder with the petroglyph, causing it to split apart. Photograph by Henry Wallace.

PETROGLYPHS AND EARTHQUAKES

One of the joys of scientific inquiry is the occasional discovery of something entirely new and unrelated to the subject at hand. In a recent study of Hohokam petroglyphs by the author and geologist James Holmlund, evidence of major prehistoric earthquakes unexpectedly presented itself. Although southern Arizona residents have little fear of earthquakes, the region's history is full of them, including a major quake in 1887. Perhaps it should not have come as a surprise, then, to discover overturned and dislodged boulders covering prehistoric glyphs, some of which had been damaged in the process. In some cases, boulders weighing a ton or more had been tossed up in the air several inches or forced both upwards and laterally.

Careful comparisons of the patina formation on the petroglyphs and that of bash marks and scrapes on boulders allowed us to develop a chronology of seismic activity. We concluded that at least two major earthquakes shook southern Arizona in prehistoric times, one at the inception of the Hohokam culture and another near the onset of the Classic period. We also found evidence of the 1887 earthquake. Our findings, combined with purely geological studies by other researchers, led us to the conclusion that major earthquakes occur at approximately one-thousand-year intervals in this region. If this is true, we need not worry for another nine centuries! This evidence is also interesting because some past earthquakes may have had a significant impact on the water sources, canals, and adobe structures of the Hohokam, not to mention their psyche.

A VANISHING LEGACY

Vandalized petroglyph panel near Phoenix. Photograph by David Noble, 1990.

Researchers continue to inventory and study Hohokam rock art. Only a few sites, including Painted Rocks State Park, west of Gila Bend, are open to the public and protected. The majority, unfortunately, are falling victim to vandalism and looting. After being illustrated in Arizona Highways magazine, the most elaborate pipette petroglyph known was stolen from a remote site. Thieves also dynamited large boulders near Phoenix to steal the petroglyphs. Many people hope that as the general public learns more about Arizona's fascinating cultural heritage, Hohokam rock art will be safer.

As rock art studies become more sophisticated and scientific, they can increasingly contribute to our understanding of the lifeways of the Hohokam, especially their belief systems and cultural values. What is more, the striking visual imagery we encounter in petroglyphs and pictographs helps us to feel a direct relationship to their creators, who have long since disappeared, and whose culture is so challenging to reconstruct.

Afterword

Emil W. Haury

ONE OF THE TRUISMS of archaeology is that wherever people settled in bygone days, whether in the tropics or in the arctic, they had to adjust to the local environment to survive. Nature's challenges to a large degree shaped human inventiveness and skills in recognizing, adapting to, and utilizing the surrounding resources. These adaptations made a direct impact on the nature and development of culture.

The Hohokam bear the distinction of having settled in the most inhospitable part of the Southwest. Their domesticates (corn, beans, squash, cotton, and perhaps a few others), the few flowing streams that traversed their terrain, and the boundless adjacent flatlands provided the ingredients for their crowning achievement: the development of many miles of irrigation canals in the Gila and Salt River valleys. The investment of labor in digging the canals and in tending the fields rooted the Hohokam to the soil. It gave them a residential stability that was directly responsible for the cultural pattern they devised, with some influential factors from Mexico, and for the development of their social and political behavior.

But let me turn the clock back to see how we, as archaeologists, have viewed the various inhabitants of the Southwest. It was not a smooth, unfaltering path that brought us to our present beliefs. The reluctance on the part of archaeologists in the 1930s to admit the word Hohokam into their vocabulary is poignantly brought out by Richard Woodbury's history of Hohokam archaeology herein. Once the idea was accepted that there could have

Excavating a Snaketown canal, 1965. Courtesy Arizona State Museum, photograph by Helga Teiwes.

been another tribal entity in the arid Southwest besides the Basketmaker-Pueblo (now known as the Anasazi), and subsequently a third with the admission of the Mogollon concept, our view of man's record in prehistory broadened to fit more in line with the multiplicity of tribes encountered historically.

Two excavations in particular are responsible for calling attention to the fact that something was brewing in the desert country that in no way could be confused with the northern Anasazi remains. The first was the Los Angeles County-Van Bergen expedition in 1929, which excavated the Grewe Site, near Casa Grande National Monument. It turned up a wealth of artifactual material unmatched in the Southwest and even attracted the attention of the London Illustrated News. The second was Gila Pueblo's work at Snaketown in 1934–35, explorations that not only netted a great quantity of material culture, but also emphasized the nature of the architecture. That research importantly provided the data for a chronology of considerable length prior to the construction of the impressive adobe ruins such as Casa Grande, to which the most attention had been paid up to that time.

It is clear to me that to understand the Hohokam it is necessary to draw a line between A.D. 1100 and 1200. During the earlier period, village houses were dispersed, and adobe was not used as a building material, but after A.D. 1200, the villages were composed of adobe compounds, within which were structures with solid adobe walls, some closely packed and multistoried. These two modes of living were totally different, and they expressed psychologically disparate attitudes on the part of the people as to how they wished to deploy themselves with respect to their neighbors. The dense, apartment-type living, in my opinion, represents an intrusion from the outside, and that building form is not to be seen as a logical evolution from the old Hohokam single-dwelling village form. Significantly bearing on this problem is the fact that after abandonment of the region by the "city-dwelling" people, those that remained behind or those that came in to reoccupy the region reverted to the open-deployment, semiunderground, fragile structures of earlier times. The tradition of adobe, pueblo-like construction did not survive into modern times as did pueblo building on the Colorado Plateau, exemplified by the Hopi and Zuni towns.

A recent stroll over the large village of Snaketown in celebration of the fifty-fifth and twenty-fifth anniversaries of my two episodes of work there vividly brought to mind lingering questions about the origin of the Hohokam: the time of their emergence or arrival, whichever was the case; their trials in coping with an austere environment; why Snaketown was abandoned about A.D. 1100; what lasting effect the possible intrusion of foreign forces had on them in close to A.D. 1200, accounting for the radical shift in architecture; what factors were at work to cause the large "towns" to be abandoned in about 1450; what stimulated the construction of the so-called platform mounds; and what, in the end, happened to the Hohokam. The preceding essays bring much light to bear on these and other problems and make clear what we know about the Hohokam in 1990. But in my candid opinion, we yet have a long way to go to fully understand their history. Regrettably, we must act fast, for the old villages and other subtle traces of Hohokam handiwork are fast disappearing beneath our society's overactive urbanization and other rearrangements of the land they once called home.

Hohokam shell bracelets. Courtesy Arizona State Museum, photograph by Helga Teiwes.

We have come a long way in our understanding of the Hohokam since the days of Cushing and Fewkes, but there still remain many vexing problems that need the attention of the researcher. Providentially, federal laws mandate that archaeological sites impacted by federally funded projects, such as canals, reservoir construction, and roads, must be excavated before development. This has greatly accelerated the study of Hohokam sites but, unhappily, given us information mainly on the later sites only. Traces of the Hohokam beginnings—their emergence, however it happened—are restricted to relatively few places such as Snaketown, and these have not played a part in the mitigation process demanded by federal law. My view is that we must concentrate on the places most likely to give us the information we need as specially designed projects, irrespective of federal intervention.

I cannot let pass this opportunity to make a few observations—perhaps my last in print—on the nature of researches into Hohokam archaeology. It is no accident that the conclusions reached about the Hohokam—their origins, when they were here, the social and political notions about them—have been more fluid and subject to more change than notions about the Anasazi. Accountable for this difference is the greater difficulty in interpreting the spread-out villages and perishable houses of the Hohokam in contrast to the close-living and solidly built, hence better preserved, remains of the Anasazi. Additionally, the proximity of the Hohokam to the Mexican high cultures adds to the complexity of reaching rational conclusions.

Demolition of a portion of the Pueblo Grande Site in 1990 prior to construction of a new freeway through Phoenix. Courtesy Phoenix Arts Commission, photograph by David Noble.

After sixty-five years of dabbling in southwestern archaeology, much of that time concerned with the Hohokam, I must freely admit that I do not see them in entirely the same light in which they are currently portrayed. First, with respect to their origin, I do not believe they are directly descended from the native Archaic antecedents. That Archaic genes may have been present in them I accept, but the difference between a site in Matty Canyon in southern Arizona in the first century B.C., with shallow pithouses, prone burials, corn, and no pottery, compared with a site dating a few centuries later, with pottery, well-developed canal irrigation, cremation, figurines, and a few other Mesoamerican analogous traits, speaks of another interpretation of early Hohokam beginnings. The cultural fabric of the Archaic and the Hohokam was not only different, but the time to effect the change appears to have been too short. Second, in archaeology, we need desperately an objective typology of "platform" mounds to show the distinction between Hohokam mounds, which I believe were ultimately related to concepts native to Mexico, and the mounds of the Salado culture, which were not only different structurally but also served a different purpose.

Clearly, then, the order of the day with respect to studying the Hohokam is to maintain an open mind, for we are a long way from having solved some of the basic problems. For that matter, I fear certain questions will always be arguable because the legacy the Hohokam left for us to decipher is lacking in certain explanatory ingredients.

With these cautions in mind, I have the temerity to declare that the accompanying papers, all written by specialists in their own right, elegantly and synoptically express what we know today about the Hohokam. Much of what is said is specific and is not likely to change; a number of thoughts voiced are speculative and in the future may be differently interpreted. This knowledge represents a truly significant advance over what we knew fifty years ago, and fifty years hence, should a new book once again review the Hohokam, I daresay we would see many new and equally marked differences in how we view these remarkably adaptable people.

Further Reading

BARTLETT, MICHAEL H., THOMAS M. KOLAZ, AND DAVID A. GREGORY
1986 *Archaeology in the City: A Hohokam Village in Phoenix, Arizona.*
The University of Arizona Press.

CROWN, PATRICIA L.
1990 "The Hohokam of the Southwest," *Journal of World Prehistory,*
vol. 4.

DITTERT, ALFRED E., JR., AND DONALD E. DOVE, EDITORS
1985 *1983 Hohokam Symposium,* Phoenix Chapter of the Arizona
Archaeological Society, Occasional Papers, no. 2, vols. I and II.

DOYEL, DAVID E.
1979 "The Prehistoric Hohokam of the Arizona Desert," *American
Scientist,* vol. 67.

FISH, PAUL R.
1989 "The Hohokam: 1,000 years of Prehistory in the Sonoran Desert,"
Dynamics of Southwestern Prehistory, edited by Linda S. Cordell and
George J. Gumerman. Smithsonian Institution Press.

GREGONIS, LINDA M., AND KARL J. REINHARD
1979 *Hohokam Indians of the Tucson Basin.* The University of Arizona
Press.

GUMERMAN, GEORGE J.
1991 *Exploring the Hohokam: Prehistoric Desert Peoples of the
American Southwest.* University of New Mexico Press.

MCGUIRE, RANDALL H., AND MICHAEL B. SCHIFFER
1982 *Hohokam and Patayan Prehistory of Southwestern Arizona.*
Academic Press.

NABHAN, GARY PAUL
1985 *Gathering the Desert.* The University of Arizona Press.
1987 *The Desert Smells Like Rain: A Naturalist in Papago
Indian Country.* North Point Press.

RUSSELL, FRANK
1908 "The Pima Indians," *Twenty-sixth Annual Report of the Bureau of
Ethnology* 1904-1905, Washington, Government Printing Office.
Reprinted 1975 by the University of Arizona Press, under the
editorship of Bernard L. Fontana.

Index